# WORKING WITH
# ADULT SURVIVORS
# OF CHILD SEXUAL
# ABUSE

Other titles in the
## Systemic Thinking and Practice Series
*edited by* David Campbell & Ros Draper
*published and distributed by* Karnac Books

# WORKING WITH ADULT SURVIVORS OF CHILD SEXUAL ABUSE

*Elsa Jones*

Foreword by
*Virginia Goldner*

**Systemic Thinking and Practice Series**

Series Editors
*David Campbell & Ros Draper*

Karnac Books

London  1991  New York

This edition first published in 1991 by
H. Karnac (Books) Ltd.
58 Gloucester Road
London SW7 4QY

Distributed in the United States of America by
Brunner/Mazel, Inc.
19 Union Square West
New York, NY 10003

ISBN 1 85575 017 1

Printed in Great Britain by BPCC Wheatons Ltd, Exeter

# CONTENTS

PART ONE

## Setting the context

## EDITORS' FOREWORD

I n 1991 professionals working in the areas of child and adult
health have to face the consequences of society's increasing
awareness of child abuse and to decide if and how they feel
able to work with either the abused or the abusers.

As editors, it seemed to us that there are already many texts
describing the pattern of child abuse and treatment plans to protect
children at risk. Not so much material is available about how to
work with adults who were abused in childhood and have lived
with the pain, confusion, shame, and guilt and the effects of these
emotions on their adult lives and relationships.

We are particularly pleased to publish this book, as not only does
Elsa Jones demonstrate the way in which systemic thinking can provide a framework for therapy with adult survivors of abuse, but she
also addresses two of the thorniest issues of the field: One, how
does a worker balance the need to explore the individual's private
experience of abuse with the need to understand the meaning of
the abuse in the larger family and social context? Two, how can a
professional take a position against the imbalance of power and

subsequent abuse, while at the same time retain enough neutrality to understand what is going on in the wider context?

Elsa Jones, who has been working from the Family Institute in Cardiff and treating adult survivors for several years, describes how she has combined systemic thinking and a feminist perspective into a theoretical model she uses to guide her work. The book has twenty case examples that convey simple descriptions of what is a complex therapeutic process.

In the book Ms Jones shares her own dilemmas about working with adult survivors, and in this way we believe the reader is offered support for the inevitable effects of the emotional impact of this work on professionals.

We are particularly pleased that the book frankly raises lots of questions. Abuse is an area of work where the knowledge of what is right and wrong often shrouds the complex issues surrounding professional decisions about what to do for the abused and abusers that is protective, preventative, and therapeutic. Through the discussion of theory and descriptions of the work, this book shows the value of making haste slowly and effectively with an emotive issue such as abuse.

*David Campbell*
*Ros Draper*
London
July 1991

# FOREWORD

I n 1895 Freud reluctantly concluded, after listening to his own patients, that they were the victims of sexual abuse within their own families. He made this discovery the cornerstone of his theory of psychopathology, writing "at the bottom of every case of hysteria there is a premature (traumatic) sexual occurrence" (*S.E., 3*, p. 203).

According to Jeffrey Masson (1986), Freud was the first man in history to document the ubiquitous, grave psychological consequences of childhood abuse. As a result, he became, in his own words, "one of those who disturbed the sleep of the world". But as Masson (1984) and others have convincingly demonstrated, the truth eventually became such a liability that Freud ultimately had to banish it from his own consciousness. Indeed, in less than two years Freud had formally repudiated what he called "the seduction theory", in favour of the victim-blaming idea that apparent memories of sexual molestation were actually the product of the unconscious childhood fantasies of hysterical women.

The psychoanalytic movement (and, by extension, the modern mental health industry) can be said to have begun with Freud's accommodation to the patriarchal pressures exerted by the bourgeois medical establishment and from within his own psyche. While it can be argued that Freud's denial of external reality resulted in his discovery of internal reality, the creation of the theory of the unconscious, the effect of his burying one truth to discover another was to consign five more generations of abused women and men to silence and shame.

Public knowledge of the reality of sexual abuse has been lost and found many more times this century. Historian Linda Gordon, documenting this process in the United States, has concluded that the fate of this dangerous knowledge, and of the victims and perpetrators whose acts and thoughts are evaluated and rendered meaningful within its categories, is tied to the upsurge and eclipse of feminist consciousness and politics. When feminism was strong, public concern about sexual exploitation grew; when feminism was weak, sexual abuse was either rendered invisible as a social problem, or fit into a new social category like "sexual delinquency", which blames the victims by criminalizing rather than pathologizing them, as Freud had done (Gordon, 1988).

David Finkelhor, a prominent researcher on the epidemiology and sociology of sexual abuse, confirms Gordon's insights about the politics of public awareness. Attention to the problem internationally is, apparently, also highly correlated with the relative strength of the women's movement in various countries. Where it is strong, incidence figures rival the shocking U.S. statistic that one in three women has been sexually abused before the age of eighteen; where the women's movement is weak, incidence figures drop, and social concern about it is minimal (Finkelhor, 1990).

What distinguishes the current period of intensified public alarm and professional discourse about sexual victimization is that, for the first time, the dimensions of the problem and the way in which it is discussed, theorized about, and "treated" have been defined by the victims themselves. In the past, although women may have put the problem on the social agenda, the professional medical and social welfare establishment defined its meaning and determined its solution. Survivors were never accorded the opportunity to corroborate, criticize, or in any way comment on what was written, taught, or done with them.

What makes things different now is that concern with the issue of sexual abuse has become a social movement. Activism transforms victims into survivors, and it is *their* voices, memories, and strategies of survival and recovery that have informed public discourse, shaped professional activity, and captured social imagination.

This development is crucial, since the crime of sexual abuse is a particularly complex and confusing kind of childhood trauma. As feminist legal scholar Catherine Mackinnon (1986) points out, it is inflicted on each victim as a member of a social group (children, females, etc.), yet, unlike other persecutions, it happens to each victim in utter isolation. Thus, like other political atrocities, sexual abuse is a collective experience, but, unlike other political atrocities, each victim believes she is alone.

It is for this reason that an adequate therapy of sexual abuse must do justice to the double injury: the injury of a particular person by a particular person or people, and the social injustice of the victim's exploitation because of the impersonal fact of her age or sex. The act of therapy often hinges on bearing witness to injustice large and small, so as to name and dignify the suffering that had to be endured alone, in silence, and without social recognition. But because the injustice of sexual exploitation transcends the personal, the clinical frame must be expanded to address the complex psycho-political nature of the abuse and victimization, including the necessity for maintaining a clear moral stance regarding responsibility and accountability.

Such a therapy not only aids the healing process of the victim, but it can also serve to advance the political process of recognition and accountability of our society as a whole. This is because as each individual therapy unfolds, as each therapist makes space for survivors to tell the whole terrible story, and to retell and rework their story from multiple perspectives, a collective narrative is being amassed: a documentary, oral history of the relational politics and human cost of sexual abuse.

Elsa Jones' fine and eloquent book, with its voluminous, richly detailed, clinically masterful case material, held in place by a morally profound, politically complex sensibility, honours that history and demonstrates the liberatory potential of reckoning with it. With remarkable lucidity and quiet authority, Jones provided us with guidelines for a therapy that matches the scope of the problem.

It is a therapy in which the systemic ideal of respectful listening and the political ideal of "gaining a voice" have been elevated to become central organizing themes of treatment. This double vision reflects the coming of age of both the systemic and the feminist traditions, as distilled in the work of a particularly gifted clinician and teacher. As a feminist, Jones insists upon locating relational dilemmas in socio-political space, in history, and within moral categories. As a systemic therapist, she demonstrates how those commitments can be met while maintaining a non-intrusive stance of curiosity, and without resorting to prefabricated formulations, explanations, interventions, or solutions. As a result, this book, and the work it describes, testifies to the healing power of a politically principled, clinically ambitious systemic therapy.

*Virginia Goldner*

**New York**
**July 1991**

# INTRODUCTION

D EFINITIONS: I will use the word "survivors" for adults who have been abused in childhood. This word is generally preferred, especially by survivors themselves, to the word "victim", which implies a static condition of being unable to escape from the abuse or its effects. Any person who reaches adulthood and comes to therapy to deal with the remaining effects of abuse is by definition a survivor, having already by implication endured and overcome major adverse experiences when young. I will use the word "abuser" as the term for the person who sexually or physically abused the child, as it seems to me the most straightforward of the various terms available.

While recognizing that both therapists and survivors may be male, I shall in general refer to therapists and clients as female.

The major focus of the book will be on working with adult survivors of childhood sexual abuse; I will, however, also at times refer to work with adults who have been physically abused in childhood, as there can be in my view some significant similarities in the effects of such abuse.

My thanks go to colleagues at the Cardiff Family Institute and elsewhere, to clients, and to workshop participants, all of whom have helped me to think more clearly and to "hear with the heart" (Malan, 1990), but most especially to B.

The Family Institute is part of Barnados' work in Wales and the South West.

# WORKING WITH ADULT SURVIVORS OF CHILD SEXUAL ABUSE

*PART ONE*

# SETTING THE CONTEXT

*CHAPTER ONE*

# Background

T he guidelines that are offered in this book were first pro-
posed by myself and my then colleague, Bebe Speed, to help
us think about work we were currently doing with women
clients who had been sexually abused as children. These ideas have
been refined and elaborated over the ensuing years as a result of
feedback from workshop attenders and clients.

There is now a wide and constantly proliferating literature on
sexual abuse, ranging from theory and research, to work with the
families of children where sexual abuse has been disclosed or
is suspected, to survivors' own accounts. My own work is firmly
based on the experience and knowledge of the many other contribu-
tors to this field (of whose work only a small selection is cited in the
bibliography). The knowledge accumulated by those working with
the disclosure, management, and therapeutic response to the sexual
abuse of children forms the bedrock on which workers with adult
survivors rest their understanding of the likely experiences and effects for their own clients. While there are—and probably always
will be—differences of interpretation and emphasis amongst those
writing about sexual abuse, there is also broad agreement, particularly amongst those working therapeutically with abused children

or adults, about the kind of helping approaches that are found useful by such clients. As Hall and Lloyd (1989) and Trepper and Barrett (1989) point out, books about therapeutic approaches (as opposed to theory) are in a minority; it has therefore seemed worthwhile to contribute my own ideas about ways of working with survivors.

These ideas are offered here, not as expert or prescriptive statements about the situation of abuse survivors, or about how they should be worked with, but purely as ideas which may offer a helpful structure for the thinking of those working in this area. There are two reasons, in particular, why I would not claim to be making an "expert" statement, and these will be discussed separately below.

## 1. A SYSTEMIC PERSPECTIVE

In the course of my teaching I all too frequently meet workers, particularly in social services agencies, who are carrying enormous case-loads of abuse work, both current and with adult survivors. It is not uncommon for such a worker to have 50 cases currently on her files. The sheer volume of this work, and its frequently distressing nature, makes it unsurprising that such workers should feel overloaded, depressed, and useless—in other words, "burnt out". In addition it is now a truism in systems thinking that professional systems often replicate the organization and characteristics of the client systems with which they work. Thus professional systems set up to deal with sexual or physical abuse can easily develop into "abusive systems", where the worker is at the receiving end of the enormous social anxiety generated by the dawning realization of the extent of abuse in our society. Such a worker will be expected to function, with no margin for error, under circumstances where her case-load is too large, where she is expected to make "life-or-death" decisions without time to think or consult, and where the media and her own hierarchy are, from her perspective, waiting to blame her for any error of judgement. She will feel abused, and her professional and personal values, her concern for clients, and her position within the hierarchy will render her voiceless, so that she is liable to blame herself for whatever goes wrong, as well as for her own unpleasant emotions. This replicates the situation of the victim of abuse.

My work in the Family Institute in Cardiff (F.I.), which will be discussed in more detail below, means that I work with abuse survivors among a range of other clients. I am therefore not an expert in abuse work, in the sense that the hypothetical worker above could be said to be, since she will have seen many more abuse survivors than I have. However, working within the team context of the Institute, and within the framework of systemic therapy, means that there is space and time to think about the problems that clients bring to therapy, which without such support can seem overwhelming. Based on this experience, it is my conviction that using the theory and skills that derive from a systemic family therapy approach is appropriate to work with abuse survivors, as with many other kinds of problem-definitions or problem-determined systems, and that thinking systemically can enable us to work with adult survivors in a way that is likely to lead to a sense of empowerment for clients and workers.

## 2. "EXPERTS" CREATE PROBLEMS

The second reason why I am reluctant to set myself up as an "expert" in work with abuse survivors is that the existence of such "expertise" would imply that having been abused as a child constituted some sort of category or syndrome, which was necessarily a source of difficulties, and which required the attention of an "expert". I agree with Durrant and Kowalski (1990) that the assumption that abuse survivors can be fitted into categories, are necessarily "damaged", and require therapy on which we are the experts, constitutes "a stance that requires clients to submit to our prescription of their experience and [we] have come to view such a process as oppressive and as potentially perpetuating the effects on self-view of the abuse itself" (p. 69). A great deal of work has been done in the attempt to define sexual abuse (and definitions differ depending on whether they emanate from abuse survivors, from mental health professionals, or seek to clarify legal categories); to establish how widespread it is; to determine whether its effects are always negative; or to discover what protective factors may be available for some abused children as compared with others. For extensive and sometimes widely differing discussions on these issues, see for example La Fontaine (1990), Hall and Lloyd (1989), Bentovim et al. (1988), or Finkelhor (1984). Until we know far more than we do at present we will not have any certainty about the incidence of childhood abuse, whether sexual or other, or of the complex, subtle, and wide-ranging consequences of having been abused. What we can do in the meantime is to work with the *experienced effects* of abuse, and to take the client's word for what these are.

I shall in the rest of this book discuss some patterns I and others have observed in our work with survivors. Because of the foregoing it should now be clear that these ideas are *guidelines* and not *blueprints* or prescriptions.

## 3. THE WORK OF THE CARDIFF FAMILY INSTITUTE TEAM

### a. Working style

The Family Institute is part of the work of Barnardos in Wales and the South West of England; it is therefore not within the Health or Statutory Services, and this fact has many implications for how this team works as compared with others. The Team consists of five family therapists and two administrative secretaries. The family therapists, who come from different professional backgrounds, work as a peer team, earn the same, and share the work of the team on a rotating basis, including the job of being Chairperson of the Institute.

The major family therapy influence on the way the F.I. team works has been the therapeutic orientation of Luigi Boscolo and Gianfranco Cecchin of the Milan Centre for the Study of the Family. We are part of a network of continuously co-evolving family therapists, which includes the two Milan men, and which is sometimes referred to as a "Post-Milan" orientation. What this means, broadly speaking, is that since the publication of the Milan group's first book (Selvini et al., 1978) numerous family therapists and teams have been taught and influenced by their way of working. In turn these groups have influenced each other as well as those members of the original Milan team who, via their teaching and consultation, have maintained links with their former trainees. This loosely linked group continues to explore the implications of new ideas, and feedback from clinical work and teaching, for both theory and practice. I shall also discuss the influence of feminist therapy and feminist critiques of family therapy on our work.

Fundamental to our work are assumptions about the way in which individuals or groups form part of evolving systems in which each individual member influences and is influenced by others. We see the therapists as participating in these systems of mutual influence, mutual search for the co-construction of new meaning, and mutual search for the possibilities of change in action or meaning. Since this is not a handbook of systemic therapy I shall not here elaborate on the complexities of theory and practice, but will illustrate the particular application to work with abuse survivors in the chapters that follow. Readers new to this way of working are referred to the reading list at the end of the book, in particular Hoffman (1981), Campbell and Draper (1985), Selvini et al. (1978), Cecchin (1987), and Jones (in press). However, I shall attempt a brief statement about some of the major components of my therapeutic orientation as a background to the work that follows, while hoping that the necessary brevity of this statement will not lead to misunderstanding.

As a therapist I assume that when someone approaches me for help with the difficulties they are experiencing these may be linked to factors both in their past and in their present, and may have individual and "internal" components as well as interactional and contextual ones. I assume that there is a looping relationship between action and meaning, so that a change in behaviour may well lead to the attribution of different meaning, just as a shift in the assumed meaning of events may lead to changes in behaviour. I assume that each individual has resources and strengths, no matter how despairing they may be feeling at the moment of coming to therapy, and that it is my job to help them find access to these, without minimizing the seriousness of the troubles by which they may have been overwhelmed. I also assume that people themselves have a better idea of their own history, values, creative resources, and what solutions are likely to fit for them, than any outsider can ever have, so that the therapist's task is, as it were, to help clients roll obstacles out of their path, but not to point out the route they should be following. At the same time I am aware, on the basis of theory as well as observations in therapy and in my own life, that it is difficult to attain an overview or meta-perspective on one's own situation, so that sitting down to talk with someone else, whether a professional therapist or not, may be necessary in order to begin to look at events, connections, and previously obscured aspects of the patterns of action and relationship that accumulate around "the problem". I therefore assume that I am unlikely to know the answers to clients' dilemmas, but that my systemic curiosity, my technical skills (e.g. in asking circular or hypothetical questions), my respectful search for their own skills and resources, my widening of the area of inquiry to include wider contexts that may previously have been left out of account, my challenge to set ways of thinking, and my attempt to create a safe and containing space in which the unthinkable and unsayable can be expressed, will have the effect of freeing up the client's own ability to explore, to grow, and to resolve dilemmas. As one client couple said to me: "Coming to sessions is fascinating: something about the way you ask questions means that we keep opening new doors that we thought weren't there." In summary I might say, then, that the therapist's major task is to introduce "news of difference" (Bateson, 1980)— that is, flexibility, complexity, options, different perspectives—into the therapeutic conversation with the client, so that the experience of being stuck and having no choice can change into one of feeling freed up to create one's own preferred new ways of relating to self and others.

What I don't assume should be implicit in the above: I do not assume the presence of pathology, with all that that concept implies about illness, defect, and the superior ability of the professional to see what is wrong and therefore to diagnose and label the client. I do not assume that it is possible to interact instructively: that is, although I may have the intention that clients should do such and so, or should interpret my words as such and so, what they in fact do with these will depend on their own history, beliefs, and values, view of the relationship with me, meaning-attribution, and so on. I do not assume that clients who do not behave in the way I expect them to, are "resistant"—instead I wonder what I may be doing to make them feel as if they've been backed into a corner, and I try to respect and understand their own style and pace of change. I assume that most people when they experience difficulties, myself included, are keen to change and anxious or fearful about the—sometimes unknown—consequences of change. I do not assume that all grief, pain, and injustice can be ameliorated, but that we may have some degree of flexibility as to the stance we adopt towards them, and that the choice of stance has implications for our well-being.

When working with clients, then, I would want to understand the difficulties and dilemmas that bring them to therapy, as well as the contexts in which these arose and are maintained, and the meanings attributed to them by the clients themselves and by others who have or have had an influence on them, such as family, friends, colleagues, or mental health professionals. While I know that the mere act of talking to someone who listens non-judgementally, and hears accurately, can be a great relief, I do not subscribe to the view that ventilation and catharsis are necessarily therapeutic, or have to precede any significant change. Therefore my focus in therapy will always be in the direction of difference, and I will be attending to the client's own descriptions of the differences they have been able to make in the past or the present to their own circumstances, as well as attempting, particularly by the use of future-oriented questions, to explore what differences may potentially occur. When a person explores hypothetical future scenarios in their own lives and those of others, the act of imagining these already alters the sense of "stuckness", in which previously no alternatives seemed possible.

I will also work in a way that attempts to empower clients. Since this is a fashionable word these days, it is necessary to explain my interpretation of it, which rests on views on the nature of the therapist/client relationship first articulated by feminist therapists (e.g. Gilbert, 1980). In order for the therapist not to abuse power it is important for her to accept that at the beginning of therapy there will be a power imbalance between herself and the client. This is because the client is the one who is seeking help, is probably feeling vulnerable and anxious, and is unsure of the "rules of the game", while the therapist is on home ground (in the sense of being familiar with the "rules" of therapy), is not participating in the therapy in order to talk about her own vulnerabilities and difficulties, and is armed with technical expertise and skill. The therapist should continue to take responsibility for the professional knowledge and experience she carries, and which she should be using and, where appropriate, sharing to the benefit of the client. She should also do all she can to shift the relationship in the direction of an open sharing between equals who are engaged in a joint venture, what Eisler (1988) calls a "partnership model".

The F.I. therapists normally work with a team and a one-way screen, as well as a videotaped record of the session. That is, the therapist is in the room with the client or clients, and one or more team members are behind a one-way screen from where they observe the therapy session, and offer comments to therapist and clients to enhance the therapeutic work. This arrangement can, of course, only be used with the permission of the client. This way of working, and its rationale, are carefully explained to clients when they first enter the room. Working in this way has proved extremely helpful to systemic therapists; therapist and clients are seen to benefit from the support and wider perspective thus obtained.

Many abuse survivors are uneasy with the presence of unseen observers, for good reasons to do with their experience, e.g. of powerlessness or of actual voyeurism. We would be particularly alert to this possibility when proposing to work with the team and with video recordings. On the other hand, some clients who have been abused welcome the presence of the team, as they regard this as offering some protection against further abuse within the therapy setting, because of the "visibility" of the therapist's work. If the client is uneasy about any aspect of our usual arrangement we would discuss a number of alternatives, ranging from no videotape, to meeting the team members who then return to their position behind the screen, to working with one team member offering live consultation in the room, to working with no team consultation at all. The case examples that are discussed, in disguised form, in this book all derive from work with clients who have given written permission for their material to be used for teaching purposes.

Our usual working format consists of brief sessions (on average between two and ten) with intervals in-between sessions ranging from one week to several months. By preference we would work with as many family members as are willing to attend sessions, together with, where relevant, other significant people such as friends, neighbours, or professional workers. When working with adult survivors we have found it necessary to combine individual meetings, that is, one-to-one therapy with the survivor, with sessions including a variety of others from the survivor's family of origin and current family. This is because much of the work requiring to be done is particularly personal and private to the survivor herself. Much of our work with survivors tends to be longer-term than our usual family therapy practice. It may be that this is because of the way in which the effects of childhood abuse tend to be intertwined with, and organizing of, most aspects of the survivor's life; on the other hand it may be due to the nature of individual therapy itself, and the therapist's assumptions about the slower pace of such work.

## b. Clients

A majority of the F.I.'s clients are self-referred. This means that they have heard of us through friends or family who have consulted us before, or have learnt of our existence from professional or community sources. The rest of the clients come to the F.I. via the usual professional referral sources. In the last few years we have seen a great upsurge in the number of adult abuse survivors coming to consult us. I know that this trend is also reflected in the work of other agencies.

Initially the majority of abuse survivors first approached the Institute in relation to problems other than those of childhood abuse, e.g. problems focused on their children, such as disciplinary issues, anorexia, or worries about over-protectiveness or sexuality. Typically, when the problem originally brought to therapy had been resolved, an adult (usually the woman) in the family would say that she would like to continue to do some work on issues "to do with myself only". As time has gone by an increasing number of adult survivors now refer directly to their childhood abuse when making the referral. The majority of adult survivors coming to us for therapy are women, but—particularly over the last few years— increasing numbers of male survivors are also coming forward.

It is obvious that, as our society has become willing to acknowledge that abuse, in particular sexual abuse, of children is widespread, so it has become possible for adults to hope that they may be believed when they decide to talk to a therapist about their childhood experiences and the consequences they now wish to alter or understand. The publicity given in the media, in schools, and in general discourse to sexual abuse, the encouragement to children to say no, are powerful incentives to survivors to risk breaking a silence that may never have been broken before. Clients report that some of the most powerful triggers—for memory or for hope— have been television documentaries or dramas. Survivors who did disclose abuse in childhood, and were disbelieved or punished, formed a powerful impression of a society in which adult consensus supported the rights of abusers, and confirmed their own sense of wrongdoing and insignificance. Now they can begin to believe that they will be heard. A colleague working in an incest telephone help-line service reports a call from a woman in her seventies who talked in some detail of the abuse she had experienced more than sixty years previously, and which she had never disclosed. When offered a counselling appointment she declined, saying that the experience of telling and being believed was one of such joy that she required nothing else.

We know from emerging evidence on child sexual abuse that the vast majority of abusers are male, and the majority of sexually abused children are female (cf. for example La Fontaine, 1990, or Haugaard & Repucci, 1988). However, male survivors of sexual abuse are increasingly approaching helping agencies; it may be that we will, in time, revise our assumptions about the gender ratio of sexually abused children. The abuse, by men, of power over women and children is coherent with the tenets of androcratic (cf. note 1) culture (see chapter two for discussion); it may be that men in this culture find it even more difficult than women to disclose sexual abuse, since the role of the victim, the one who is helpless and gets used for another's gratification, does not sit comfortably with cultural expectations of male roles.

## c. Gender of therapist

When we first started working with adult survivors (cf. note 2), our first few female clients expressed a preference for seeing a female therapist. We therefore worked with them with a female therapist in the room, and a female consultant behind the screen (when a consultant was used). This chimed with our own views at the time. The female team members felt quite strongly that it was appropri-ate, not only to accede to the client's request, but that even if such a preference was not expressed it might be better for the therapist to be a woman.

In addition, our male colleagues expressed unease about working with women who had been sexually abused by men. Many male therapists have since expressed the view that it is very difficult for a man to do this kind of work well. Given that most sexual abuse is perpetrated by males against females, many male therapists are sensitive to the need not to repeat abusive power relationships within the therapist/client relationship. They fear that the presence of a male therapist, combined with the unavoidable authority and power imbalance that exists in virtue of the therapist's professional role, will reinforce the woman's experience of being powerless. Female clients may already have experienced further abusive relationships with therapists (cf. note 3). In addition, male therapists talk of the stress and shame occasioned in them by having to represent the gender that has been responsible for so much violence.

The opinion is sometimes expressed by therapists that a woman survivor who expresses a preference for working with a female therapist should be "persuaded" to work with a man. They argue that the experience of learning to trust a "good man" will be a powerful therapeutic corrective for her. This seems to me a most tendentious view. Even if we can be certain that the therapist is able to represent such an ideal figure (cf. note 3), the attitude that wishes the client to submit to something she does not want, that will be "good for her", seems uncomfortably close to the situation she has probably already experienced when being abused.

Nevertheless, if women therapists, working alone or within team context, are to become the only ones able to see abuse survivors, male or female, this will rapidly lead to a situation of "ghettoization" for therapists and clients. Female therapists will find that their case-loads become overwhelmingly filled with abuse work, which will deprive them of widening the range of their practice, which is essential if burn-out is to be avoided. At the same time male therapists will not confront the difficult issues necessary to free them up for work with adult survivors. It is therefore important for male therapists, in co-operation with female colleagues or in male-only groups, to work to increase their gender-sensitivity to the point where this therapeutic work can safely be expected to lead to a sense of self-control and empowerment for male and female clients.

# CHAPTER TWO

# Feminism and family therapy

O ver recent years family therapists, like therapists working in other modalities, have subjected their theories and practices to the critical lens of feminist thought (e.g. Goldner, 1985, 1988, 1991; Hare-Mustin, 1986; Pilalis, 1987; Perelberg & Miller, 1990). It would be over-optimistic to claim that these critiques have now so transformed systemic therapy that sensitivity to problems of power or gender imbalance in families are part and parcel of the thinking of family therapists. Nevertheless, the increasing awareness of feminist critiques, and the light they throw on evolving systemic theory and practice, have enabled us to begin to think more clearly about certain previously obscured aspects of our work.

Throughout most of the world, and certainly in the West, we have for several thousand years lived in androcratic cultures. This has major implications, not only for the lives of our clients and ourselves, but also for the theories and practices that will evolve within these cultures. It is therefore axiomatic that systemic therapy (indeed any therapy) will embody certain principles pertaining to the maintenance of the androcratic status quo; moreover, these organizing principles will normally be *invisible* to us. The papers, books, workshops, discussions, and battles between colleagues that have been informed by feminist critiques have been part of the process of allowing us as therapists to begin to acknowledge the significance, firstly, of the cultural/political system within which we live, and secondly, of the influence of gender roles on ourselves and our clients.

## 1. THE INFLUENCE OF ANDROCRATIC CULTURE

I do not propose here to argue the case for the existence of androcracy, or its intimate association with ideas and practices of dominance, exploitation, and violence. Unconvinced readers may wish to read, among a wealth of possible references, Eisler (1988), Morgan (1989), Smith (1989), and Spender (1980). I will, rather, consider the implications of androcracy for the experiences and socialization of abuse survivors.

In our culture imbalances in power exist within relationships, and are frequently exploited to the benefit of the more powerful. Slave-owning, torture, and war are blatant examples of such exploitation, but many other examples are hidden under the guise of "normal life". For example, in Britain it is not yet considered wholly unacceptable for adults to use their greater physical strength to beat children—though a child may well be beaten for hitting a smaller child! The campaign to stop corporal punishment in schools has had an uphill struggle to convince parents and teachers of the unacceptability of institutionalized violence in schools. The designation of violence within a male–female couple as "domestic" (and therefore not to be responded to by the police with the same degree of seriousness as they would employ when dealing with violence between strangers), and the recent debate about the legal difficulties encountered when attempting to recognize the concept of rape within marriage, are further examples of the acceptance of certain kinds of violence within our society. We defend ourselves against knowing about these common features of our world by claiming that these sorts of incidents, when discussed, are either exaggerated or exceptional. We need to recognize that they are neither: they are a logical expression of the values of our culture (see e.g. Penfold & Walker, 1984; Mitchell, 1985).

The Western nuclear family, among its many functions, some of which are arguably now obsolete, serves to provide a "haven in a heartless world" (for the male breadwinner), and to rear and socialize children. The family is typically seen as a private domain, a place with a boundary around it, into which outsiders do not readily intrude without invitation. Children, in our culture, are expected to obey adults, who are seen to know more about right and wrong. When a child in a family that operates by these "rules" is abused, she may remain very confused as to whether her abuse is a deviation from or a further logical expression of a social organization in which the needs of the adult (male) come first, and in which the sanctity of family life predominates.

## 2. THE INFLUENCE OF GENDER ROLES

It can be argued that the emphasis on gender differences serves to obscure the great similarities between women and men as members of the same species, and that such an emphasis serves the interests of androcracy. In a culture that follows a "dominator" model (Eisler, 1988), difference all too often means inferior or superior. Nevertheless differences do exist, and psychologists and sociologists have puzzled mightily as to which differences are innate and which the product of culture. We are unlikely to find clear answers to this question until we have a significantly different culture. In the meantime it is clear that in a dominator culture gender differences, whether innate or learned, serve to advantage or disadvantage those displaying the attributes of their gender. In the same way other differences, such as colour or ethnic or religious affiliation, are used as signifiers for power or discrimination.

Some of the gender role attributions and expectations that impinge significantly on the lives of abuse survivors are embedded within the culture in such a way that they can be difficult for therapists—who are socialized by the same cultural processes as their clients—to see. This then allows therapists to continue to take certain ideas about roles for granted, render them invisible, or to play the game of "blame the victim". For example, therapists may assume, in common with family members, that the emotional well-being of children is primarily the responsibility of the mother; if it does not occur to the therapist to question her own assumptions in this regard, she is also unlikely to enable family members to question these assumptions and their effects on family functioning. Other gender roles, and their influence on the perceptions of therapists and lives of clients, may be more visible but can remain hard to deal with given the general therapeutic prejudice against behaving "politically", which will be discussed later. For example, it may be obvious to all that a father in a family uses his greater physical strength to intimidate others, but the therapist may be afraid that asking questions about this, expressing a view about the unacceptability of violence, or offering the number of the women's refuge may be seen as intruding unacceptable personal values into the "neutral" context of therapy.

Some gender role assumptions, myths, or traditions that influence whether abuse takes place, whether it is disclosed, whether the discloser is believed, ignored, or punished, and how professional workers respond to survivors and members of their families, will be mentioned briefly:

1. The belief that male sexuality is a "force" which must be satisfied:   This belief is held by abusers, who regard their own "needs" as predominating over the wishes, welfare, or even life of the person they wish to abuse sexually. This belief is also deeply embedded in our culture—see for example the problems, mentioned above, regarding the acknowledgement of the existence of rape within marriage.

2. The belief that mothers are responsible for what happens in families:   Our culture assumes that relationships are "women's business", and child-rearing remains an almost exclusively maternal responsibility, despite the recent appearance of the so-called "new man". This means that abuse perpertrators, children who are being abused, *and therapists* will often think of the abuse in such a manner that the mother is blamed—for not preventing the abuse, for not knowing about it, for colluding with it, or, most perniciously , for provoking it by e.g. depriving her husband of sex (cf. no. 1 above and chapter six). An interesting offshoot of this and related beliefs about the "nature" of women

is the shock usually expressed when a woman is identified as the perpetrator of, or collaborator with, sexual abuse of a child; our response says something about our assumptions about both women and men. While it is true that women are in a minority within the group of abusers, it is nevertheless true that they may abuse children sexually. Sometimes this evidence is rejected, as if all women must measure up to the idealized fantasy of the nurturing mother; on the other hand, some respond with glee to this evidence and exaggerate the significance of the figures, as if the presence of some female abusers cancels out the predominance of male abusers.

3. The belief that children are seductive, tell lies about being abused, and fantasize sexual actions with adults (cf. La Fontaine, 1990, for an excellent discussion of these issues):   This is a belief that sustains those who are horrified and overwhelmed by the growing evidence for a high incidence of abuse. While the entire research field cannot be summarized here, it may be useful to bear in mind that the general indication from research evidence suggests that young children have not been found to lie when they make allegations of abuse. Where unfounded accusations have been made, these have mainly fallen into two categories: adults have been suspicious without due cause, or told lies and persuaded children to back them up (most commonly in the process of custody disputes), and children who have previously been abused have told lies about a recurrence of the abuse, primarily in situations where they were afraid that contact with the abuser was about to be re-established.

4. The belief that men have ownership of the members of the household:   The view that the man is the head of the household, that men may exchange women and children's bodies with other men, and that a man may do as he wishes within the sanctity of his own home goes back into antiquity and is enshrined in most of the dominant religious texts of the world. The attitude underlying practices that may now be diminishing is not obsolete and may be observed in our laws, cultural and marriage practices, jokes, and social conventions. It is not surprising, therefore, if in such a context an abusing father expresses the view that all the female or young flesh in the family belongs to him; that if one

woman is not available to him, due to illness, pregnancy, death, or unwillingness, the next one will be taken as substitute.

5.  The belief that might is right, and the support this view receives from cultural and social institutions.

6.  The belief that women exist to serve (and service) men:    This is a belief likely to be held by both father and mother, abuser and would-be protector(s) of the child. It is likely to influence the relationships between all parties. A mother may have learnt this lesson in her family of origin, through being abused or watching her mother being abused, or through her general learning of the cultural injunctions that inform the socialization of women and of men. This will interfere with her ability to protect her daughter, who will then absorb the same lesson. Until women can free themselves from this belief they will continue to be vulnerable to the abuse of power in one form or another.

## 3. PROBLEMS IN FAMILY THERAPY

The field of family therapy, and in particular of the systemic approaches with which I associate myself, is undergoing an apparently constant process of change. Some of this change is consequent on the nature of systemic theory and practice. An approach that views meaning as observer-created, that does not presume to search for "the one truth", but regards the world of relationships as a multiverse (Maturana, 1988), and which sees adaptation and responsiveness to feedback as cornerstones of its way of working, must by its nature continue to evolve. However, some of the changes currently being thought about are happening in response to feminist critiques of the ideas and the practice of systemic family therapy.

Family systems therapy started out from the premise that a family (or other groups of people who were meaningfully connected with one another over time) could be described as a system of mutually interacting relationships, in which people influenced each other and were in turn influenced, and where these relationships and influences developed patterning over time. As time passes, any body of theory, no matter how elegant or tentative it may have been originally, tends to become reified and oversimplified. Ideas that were part of a complex set of mutually balancing propositions become slogans, metaphors become facts, suggestions that produced good results once become rules. In my view, some of the feminist critique of family therapy relates to these "bad habits", whereas others refer to more serious inadequacies within the field itself, such as the struggle that systemic theorists and therapists are having in coming to terms with issues of power and the abuse of power. For a wider discussion, see Goldner (1985, 1988), Perelberg and Miller (1990), and Jones (in press).

An example of a "bad habit" would be the way in which ideas about the mutuality of influence in families become, under the pressure of practice, beliefs that all family members exert equal power or have equal choice in families. In other words, therapists, when taking the time to have a theoretical discussion, might be well aware that the concept of circular interaction does not imply an equivalence or identity between the relative degrees of influence attributed to or brought to bear by different participants; however, when seeing one family after another, and developing a jargonistic shorthand with which to communicate rapidly with colleagues, they may well find themselves, over time, acting within the therapeutic setting as if this equivalence exists. An example might clarify the foolishness of this view. When a first baby is born, the existence and presence of the baby exerts an enormous influence on the couple and many others to whom they relate. The baby transforms a pair of lovers into parents, their parents into grandparents, and may alter the meaning of, and balance within, relationships. The couple's relationships to the world of work, sleep, friends, and money change because of the arrival of the baby. If the baby does not sleep well, the parents will feel exhausted, desperate, inadequate, and completely powerless. Nevertheless it would be nonsense to say that the baby has equal power or influence in the family when compared to the parents. The parents can love or neglect, feed or starve, cuddle or kill the baby, and the baby will not be able to prevent them. Their decisions, whether trivial or significant, will combine to shape the course of the baby's life in a way that is different from the influence the baby's presence has on the shape of their lives. That is, there is a complementary reciprocity between parents and baby, but they do not dispose of equal influence or freedom of choice within the family.

When working with problems of mutual interdependence that are, perhaps, less obvious than this example, family therapists have sometimes made the error of assuming an equal voice for each family member. This is particularly easy to do when looking at the adults in the family, so that for example in sexual abuse work therapists who have been keen not to adopt a simplistic blaming stance towards a father who has sexually abused his children will instead end up blaming the mother. They will act on the assumption that she has an equal voice, without considering the cultural beliefs discussed above, which, together with financial constraints and physical fear, may make her unable to assert her choices in the family to the same extent that her male partner does.

One of the cornerstones of systemic family therapy practice is the idea of "neutrality" (cf. Selvini et al., 1980; Cecchin, 1987). This is a much misunderstood term, which has sometimes been interpreted as prescribing a cold, distant analytic attitude on the part of the therapist. At its best it describes a therapeutic stance of systemic curiosity (Cecchin, 1987) which means that the therapist wants to explore, together with the client, how things come to be the way they are, and how they might be different, without prescribing norms or goals to the client. It also implies an even-handedness in relation to all family members, so that the therapist attempts to hear all the different points of view, without taking one or the other side. The therapist may, as a human being, not be neutral (that is, lacking a point of view) towards the suffering or inflicting of pain, but will not attempt to impose either her personal emotional reactions, or her preferred solutions, onto clients.

However, in theory as well as in practice, the idea of systemic neutrality has created many difficulties for therapists who strive towards anti-sexist and anti-racist practice (i.e. a practice that does not pretend to a "neutrality" that in fact upholds a status quo that disadvantages some and privileges others), and who therefore recognize the necessity of including an awareness of inequity and power abuse in their work with clients. Perhaps more than any other client group, sexually abused children have confronted systemic therapists with the need to find a way of acknowledging the facts of violence and abuse, without losing the valuable perspective that systemic ideas about circularity, context, and pattern have brought to their work.

In my view these difficulties in part relate to another reification: that of the idea of the family as "the system". Family therapy's recognition that an individual's behaviour or symptoms occurred within a context of history, relationships, and meanings was a significant contribution to the field of therapy. However, it is as if family therapists then forgot that families and their difficulties also exist within a context of history, relationships, and meanings. It is then important for us to remember that we are unlikely to have useful conversations with clients, or assist them in thinking clearly and flexibly about their situation and how they might want to change it, unless we also discuss with them the historical, cultural, and socio-economic contexts within which they live (cf. also part three).

## 4. INTERACTION BETWEEN FEMINIST AND SYSTEMIC PRACTICE

Cornerstones of feminist therapy have been the idea that the "personal is political", and that the therapist should work in such a way as to empower the client and establish an egalitarian relationship within therapy. (For a more extended discussion see, e.g., Gilbert, 1980; Jones, 1990; or Lewin, 1990.) Systemic therapy has also been moving in a direction that seeks to demystify the therapist/client relationship (Andersen, 1987; Hoffman, 1990), via the use of "reflecting" teams, ideas of "conversation", "co-construction", and "partnership models" (Eisler, 1988; Hoffman, 1990). The aim is to move away from earlier ways of working, whose metaphors were often those of combat, where the therapist remained a powerful and often mysterious and devious figure, towards a style of working where therapist and client cooperate to discover *the client's* meanings and goals for change.

Thus while the idea of a more empowering relationship makes for an easy fit between the two approaches of feminism and systems therapy, there has been more of a gulf between them in relation to the idea that "the personal is political". Thus it has been suggested (Lewin, 1990) that systemic thinking is inherently a-political or anti-political, whereas feminist therapy is by its nature wedded to political action and therefore incapable of taking the whole mutually

interacting system into account. I do not see such a vast gulf between the two stances of "systemic curiosity" on the one hand, and
feminist commitment to exposing the oppressive nature of female
experience on the other. Humm (1989) says, "when women understand that their individual experience of male violence has an objec-
tive social basis and social origin, they are making feminist theory".
Yes, and they are also gaining a large-systemic perspective on their
individual experience.

# PART TWO

# GUIDELINES

As was stated in part one of this book, the guidelines presented in the chapters below are meant to serve exactly as that—they are suggestions, not blueprints. To some extent they are presented in rough chronological order, i.e. in the order in which they are likely to be dealt with in therapy. For example, it is unlikely that issues of the client's own role in the system in which abuse occurred could be explored unless she has accepted the idea that she is not to blame for what happened. However, this does not imply that any of these areas can be so neatly dealt with that something occurring in, say, chapter four will not recur again in, say, chapter six. The guidelines have been created to help the therapist have some structure in her head, a map with which she can find her way in a situation of great complexity. The territory to which the map relates is, as always, far more multidimensional than the simple lineal guidelines of the map. Matters described under one or other heading will be interlinked, will recur in different shapes, and will gain richness from being considered in relation to different aspects of the client's past, present, and future.

# CHAPTER THREE

# Hearing the relevant account

Someone who was abused in childhood is likely to have had experiences convincing her that others do not want to know about what happened to her. She may have tried to tell various people, only to be met with disbelief, incomprehension, outrage, or "deafness". She is likely to have formed the opinion that she is to blame for what happened (cf. chapter four), and to doubt the ability of others to accept her if they knew her history. She may indeed have been told by her abuser that she is to blame, that it is her wickedness, seductiveness, and so on that is responsible for his sexual behaviour; she may also have had responses of horror and rejection from others when disclosing the abuse. These and similar experiences will make her very cautious in therapy about telling the full account. She will be monitoring the therapist's responses with all the subtlety and cautiousness at her command, to assess whether it is safe for her to tell more, or whether she should withhold further detail.

A not uncommon situation in therapy might be the following: a client seems to have told all the relevant details of her experience. The therapist therefore judges that it may now be appropriate to

27

move on to other topics, to begin to consider how these experiences play a part in the client's current life, to attend to issues of the client's self-esteem, to consider how past and present relationships are linked in with the abuse, and so on. However, the therapy gets "stuck", therapist and client seem at an impasse, it feels to the therapist as if the client is mistrustful, sad, or resigned.

After some time the client may begin to talk about further and more destructive and "disgusting" details of how she was abused. It becomes clear to both therapist and client that the "stuckness" had to do with a sense on the client's part that she could not risk telling the therapist about further abuse, for fear that if the therapist really knew (and, by implication, really knew "what the client was like") she could not continue to be as accepting of the client as she had heretofore seemed to be. For the client it feels like being between the devil and the deep blue sea: if she does not take the risk of letting the therapist know everything that seems relevant to her, she cannot test out the possibility of being acceptable to others and to herself, despite what was done to her and the concomitant feelings of shame and disgust she has retained. On the other hand, telling the therapist more may risk rejection, thus confirming her childhood conviction (and perhaps her childhood experience) that she has become unacceptable in consequence of the abuse.

The client's cautiousness may well be reinforced by the therapist's reluctance to hear too much detail. For the therapist, hearing an account of violent or bizarre sexual acts may well be disturbing. The therapist may be struggling with emotions of sadness, horror, anger, helplessness, disgust at being in a "voyeuristic" situation, and so on; her desire not to have to hear any more will be picked up by the client, and interpreted in the light of her own fears (Booth, 1988).

It is therefore crucial that the therapist should signal her willingness to hear *as much as the client considers to be relevant*, in order not to block the narration of significant experiences. However, this equally means that the therapist should recognize and respect the client's view that she has said enough and does not need to give further detail. Just as in the scenario above, where the therapist prevents the client from discussing detail, so the therapist may, because of her own assumptions about what is necessary, undermine the client's trust and autonomy by insisting that every detail of the abuse must be told. In such a situation the client is likely to feel abused again.

For many clients it is not necessary to recount their experiences of abuse in any detail. They may already have done this with others (therapists, friends, or partners), or it may not serve a useful purpose for them now. The therapist needs to maintain the sort of open and respectful attitude that can accept the client's judgement, while continuing to indicate a willingness to hear more, if the client judges this to be relevant. Such acceptance and/or willingness may be indicated by the asking of open-ended, hypothetical, or "point-of-view" questions, e.g. "If there were more that you felt it was important for me to know about, what would make it easier for you to tell me about it?"; "How will you know when you have talked enough about the detail of what happened, and can now leave it behind you?"; "If you were hesitating about telling me more, because you were worried that I might be shocked or upset, what could I say or do that might make it safe for you to continue?" A therapist is more likely to be able to do this if she has colleagues with whom she can discuss, not only her handling of the case, but her own emotional responses. These colleagues may be "live" consultants, or they may be fellow workers in the same agency or elsewhere; the important issue is that therapists *and their employers* should acknowledge the need for support and space to talk.

*CHAPTER FOUR*

# The question of blame
# and responsibility

I n working with adult survivors it seems to me important, as
early in the therapy as is practicable, to make a clear statement
about the issue of blame and responsibility. This comes from
the experiences of colleagues working with children who have
been or are being abused. It may not seem like a major issue to readers
who are not systemic family therapists; however, within the family
therapy community this statement initially elicited some criticism.
It seemed to family therapists not possible to make such an apparently "lineal" statement, while still retaining the possibility of working "neutrally" with all family members, and while intending to
consider the parts played by all family members within the system
within which abuse occurred. In my experience it has indeed been
possible to combine these two apparently incompatible attitudes.

Within the first or second session, once at least an outline of the
childhood abuse has been given, I will look for the opportunity to
say the following: "There is something I want to say to you, which is
based on my experience and that of many other colleagues working
with the children who have been sexually abused. When a sexual
act happens between an adult and a child, *regardless of what the child*

*may have done*, the child is not to blame. It is the adult who is responsible for what has happened." I will then expand on this by saying that in our culture children are taught that they must obey adults; they learn that when something uncomfortable happens between adult and child the usual interpretation is that it is the child who has been naughty.

It is important to stress that this statement holds regardless of the child's actions. Clients who have been held responsible for the abuse in the past (cf. chapter three), clients who see themselves as having sought out the affection of the abuser, or who have been abused by a number of different people, will consider that they are the exception to this rule unless the unconditionality of the statement is stressed.

Clients will not necessarily accept this statement when first hearing it; indeed they may vigorously dispute it. I will then maintain, firmly but non-dogmatically, that this is my view, based on my experience and beliefs. Sometimes clients allow the statement to pass without any comment, but return to it again and again in the course of the therapy, either because for them it did have a liberating effect, or because their inability to absolve themselves of blame is central to the difficulties with which they are struggling.

*Example 1:*   A woman who had been sexually abused from the age of five by a neighbour held the firm opinion that she was responsible for the continuation of the abuse because she had accepted sweets from him on each occasion. She had concluded, at that young age, that she must be a person of little worth, since she was willing to do something that disgusted her, for such a paltry" reward". She returned in session after session to my "no-blame statement"; she considered that it might well be true for most other abused children but did not apply to her. Since the abuser did not live in her house, she also considered that it had been in her power to avoid him. She held these views despite the fact that, from my point of view, her family circumstances and the position and behaviour of the abuser gave her little choice. As therapy continued it became clear that this self-judgement, that she had made at such a young age, had coloured her entire life, so that none of her considerable achievements counted for anything in her opinion. In the course of therapy she lifted this "filter" of worthlessness through which she had viewed all her actions. It was only as she became more able to value herself, and to give herself some credit for having survived extremely difficult circumstances (in addition to the sexual abuse), that she finally began to indicate some willingness to concede the validity of my statement. It seems to me that our discussion of this statement, at her instigation, in almost every therapy session, as well as her struggling with it between sessions, constituted an important part of the therapeutic work.

While in some situations, such as the example above, the statement about blame and responsibility may well remain a "live" issue throughout most of the therapy, in general it needs to have been dealt with before proceeding to the next steps. For example, a client who continues to feel overwhelmingly to blame for the abuse will find it difficult to clarify her views about the abuser, or to consider her own part in the relevant system. However, even clients who accept the "no-blame" statement with relief early on in therapy may return to it at various stages as they review the progress they have made. One survivor, in her last therapy session, said: "I feel I know that child (i.e. her earlier self) so well now—I've actually seen her, I've felt her, I've heard her, I've seen how she fought. That was good for me because I thought . . . I could understand how I must have tried. I've seen how he just thought nothing of me, and *he* was the one that did that, not me, *he* was the one, and I could see that. I was saying let me free, and he was saying no. So *he* was the guilty partner, not me."

# CHAPTER FIVE

# The relationship with the abuser

Each survivor will have a different perspective on the importance of her relationship with the abuser, and how this has affected, and perhaps continues to affect, her views of herself and others. This perspective will be influenced by many factors, some of which will be idiosyncratic. However, the nature of the relationship preceding the abuse may make a difference to the impact that the abuse had; for instance, some researchers suggest that the closer the relationship between abuser and abused, the more likely it is that the abuse will be experienced as severely harmful, e.g. as in father–daughter incest. There are also more pervasive effects, such as those discussed in sections 3 and 4 below, which depend less on whether the abuser is a father or a stranger, and more on the kind of message the child receives about the acknowledgement or invalidation of their experiences by the adult world.

## 1. THE ABUSER AS OUTSIDER

How central this area is to the course of the therapy will depend partly on the formal and emotional relationship between the abuser and the child. In situations where the abuser was someone outside the child's significant relationships—a stranger, a neighbour, a new step-parent whom the child disliked from the word go—the survivor may, long before coming into therapy, have relegated this person to an unambivalent position in their world of relationships. I see no reason why I should attempt to change the views of a survivor who has decided, to her own satisfaction, that her abuser was an unmitigated villain. It is not my business to try to persuade her to adopt a more "systemic" or compassionate view of this person's background, constraints, and so on. Her preoccupations are likely to be directed towards the behaviours and relationships of others in her immediate circle at the time, and this will then determine the focus of therapy.

## 2. THE ABUSER AS "SIGNIFICANT OTHER"

However, for many survivors the abuser was someone with whom they had a multi-faceted relationship. One of the consequences of such a relationship is that the meaning of the abuse will have become interwoven into many aspects of relationship and self-definition. This is because abuse by someone whom the child has trusted, perhaps continued to love, and continued to be in daily contact with throughout her childhood, with all the opportunities for ambivalence that are implied in such a long-term interaction, will have affected her views of herself and her own value as a person, her sexuality, her judgements, or her capacity in adulthood to keep herself or her children safe. In therapy, therefore, she may wish to re-evaluate, as an adult, how she remembers and now views her abuser: she may, for example, have held on to a dream that he would turn out to be a good father after all, if only she could find the key. She may therefore, in the course of therapy, reach a point of accepting that he will not, at this date, become different, that the way he is is not her fault, and that she has a choice between differentiating between his "good" and "bad" bits, or of giving up her dream of a perfect father waiting to be elicited by her efforts. Some survivors are afraid that, because they continue to value or love aspects of the abuser, they will be judged as having colluded with the abuse. Others no longer trust their own judgement or capacity to protect themselves, and therefore avoid all closeness. The aim in therapy will be to make these beliefs and attitudes available for re-examination, so that the survivor's perception of the abuser can be separated out from her responses to the rest of the world and to herself.

*Example 2:*   Ms A had spent the first two years of her life passed from pillar to post between her mother and a variety of homes and foster placements, before she finally went to live with her grandparents. In her memory her grandmother was a cold and distant woman, of whom both she and her childlike grandfather were afraid. Her grandfather was the first person—and until she left home to get married at sixteen, the only person—who gave her any affection. He nurtured her, played with her, saw to her comfort, loved her—and he abused her sexually. The abuse was of such a nature that although she felt uncomfortable about it even when very young, and resisted it forcefully when older, it was nevertheless never violent or directly frightening. She also experienced physical pleasure at times.

The combination of her grandfather as the only loving person throughout her childhood, and the involuntary physical responses she had experienced while being abused, had continued to cause great problems in her life subsequently, and now became a major issue in therapy. She had found herself unable to trust anyone who behaved lovingly towards her, while at the same time fearing that the only alternative to submitting to relationships that were bound to be abusive was to live a lonely and loveless life. Whenever she experienced sexual pleasure with a partner, she would have a "flashback" in which she would be overwhelmed by images, sensations, and memories of her grandfather's sexual acts. She felt betrayed by her body, and this had become the basis of her negative self-judgement. The only way in which she could allow herself to experience sexual pleasure was to make herself so drunk beforehand that it was as if she was not really participating in the act.

A large part of the therapeutic work for Ms A consisted in reviewing her life with her grandfather in some detail, so that she eventually felt able to separate his "loving self" from his "abusing self". It was important for her to be able to acknowledge the good things she had received from him, the more so as he had provided her only childhood experience of love. She was able to view him in the context of what she knew about his background, relationships with the rest of the family, and his very limited and immature functioning as a "pseudo-adult" who, in her mature judgement, had looked to her for comfort precisely because she was a child, and in a sense nearer to his own emotional age. She could therefore hold on to her knowledge that what he had done to her sexually was unacceptable, while not having to destroy what continued to be of value for her in her memories of him. These explorations in the course of therapy were combined with factual discussions about the nature of the physiological sexual response; this was not new information for Ms A, but it became possible for her to acknowledge what she knew, and to forgive her body for its "betrayal", only in the context of the changed perspective on her grandfather. The way in which attitudes towards her grandfather and attitudes towards her own sexuality had been intertwined before meant that for her to have accepted her own sexuality with pleasure would have carried the implication of condoning grandfather's acts.

## 3. THE ENTITLEMENT NOT TO BE ABUSED

It is important for an abuse survivor to be supported in arriving at the conviction that *she is entitled not to be abused*. Whatever the abuser's circumstances, whatever grave sins and failings the survivor may want to accuse herself of, whatever excuses others have put forward, the bottom line is that each individual is entitled not to be abused. The way in which the therapist talks with the client—her respect for the client's views, her encouragement of the client's judgements of self-worth—forms part of the process through which the survivor will strengthen her sense of her own dignity and right to an inviolate life. This means that the therapist will encourage the survivor to recognize her anger at the abuse she suffered. This anger will not necessarily be expressed to the abuser—indeed, in the case of many survivors all contact with the abuser has been lost. The value that such anger has lies particularly in its relation to the survivor's sense of self-worth.

*Example 3:* Ms B related a "flashback" experience: "I can see myself in a little white dress. I was crying for him to leave me alone: 'Please, please leave me alone. I want to go to Mummy', and I was begging and crying, and he wouldn't listen to me. 'No. no', he said 'Daddy's got to do this'. I remember screaming and crying, so it must have been early on, because when I got a bit older I just was passive and withdrawn into myself; so it must have been pretty early on, because I was obviously still fighting then till I realized it wasn't worth it." As she relates this to the therapist, her voice tone and posture change, she looks and sounds much more assertive, and she goes on to say: "But I was begging him, and the feeling of the lack of self-worth that came up with that child then—no, you're nothing, you were just nothing, you were just there to be used, 'I've got to do it'. I realized where all my self-worth—the lack of it—stemmed from. It was a devastating pain, absolutely. I thought, God, the anger then! As an adult . . . oh, if I'd got him then I would have smashed him. I want to kill that man!"

Whether this anger is translated into direct action in relation to the abuser or other family members is a matter for individual judgement. However, this judgement will be easier to make when the survivor has been able to find her voice and her just rage within the safe space of the therapeutic relationship.

## 4. LIVING IN DOUBLE REALITY

In my view one of the major negative consequences of being abused as a child lies in the confusion generated for the child between what she knows to be true and what her world acknowledges to be true (for a brilliant and disturbing "fictional" treatment cf. Dworkin, 1990). This applies as much to those who have experienced physical abuse as it does to those who have been subjected to sexual abuse. The child's reality is one in which she knows what happens between her and the abuser, she knows what her physical and emotional sensations are, she knows her sense of the wrongness of the events and the relationship. At the same time the adult "real" world around her denies this truth. Parents, neighbours, or figures of authority in the community may relate to the abuser as to someone worthy of respect. Indeed, the abuser's public persona may be respectworthy. Since the child is likely, in all other respects, to be receiving an upbringing that conveys the message that what adults say is true, she is left with considerable confusion between, so to speak, what she knows she knows, and what she does not (or cannot be allowed to) know she knows. For example, her private knowledge may mean that she has seen her mother's face distort with rage and sadistic laughter when she is being beaten, whereas all the adults and other children in her world speak with admiration and affection of her mother as a wonderful nursery school teacher.

The consequence of this sort of experience, repeated again and again, is that the child finds herself living in two worlds. Considerable clinical observation has suggested that one of the ways that survivors cope with abuse—and, I would suggest, with the experience of two incompatible "truths"—is to split their awareness. This phenomenon is not new, and has been noted by many therapists (e.g. Blake-White & Kline, 1985; Booth, 1988; Courtois, 1988; Gil, 1988; Gilligan & Kennedy, 1989; McGee et al., 1984). Masson (1988) also discusses the speculations of Sandor Ferenczi and Robert Fliess around this idea. This style of dealing with incompatible or unassimilable experiences, and the ways in which this mode of dealing with the world manifested itself, was often labelled as "hysterical". We need only remember that some of Freud's early clients, from whose case histories this terminology derives, were in fact sexually abused (Masson, 1984, 1988; La Fontaine, 1990). The shame of the therapeutic community who for so long attributed clients' accounts of sexual abuse to infantile sexual fantasy is of course a topic that at long last is receiving an airing.

Thanks to the contributions of Ericksonian therapists (e.g. Erickson & Rossi, 1976; Booth, 1989, 1990), we are now able to recognize, firstly, that all of us have the capacity to split off attention when necessary—e.g. if you are finding this book interesting you will have become oblivious to extraneous noises while reading, but you will register when your child calls you or the kettle boils; and, secondly, that this may be a capacity or talent highly developed in abuse survivors, since the ability to do so may well have been a significant component of the capacity to survive at all.

*Example 4:* Ms C described how, when her step-father was abusing her, she visualized a small black coffin, lined with white satin, which was inside her chest. She would place her "real self" in the coffin and close the lid whilst the abuse continued. When the time was right in therapy, signalled in part by the vividness with which these memories returned, we agreed that the coffin was no longer the right place for the real C. Instead, she decided that she would like to place her abuser in the coffin and consign him to oblivion. We talked this through in great detail, including the colour and material of the coffin, how his effigy would feel to the touch, how the lid would be nailed shut, where and how the coffin would be disposed of. We agreed that it was not the real man, who might or might not be wandering around somewhere in the real world, who was being nailed into the coffin, but the mental image of him that she had been carrying all these years. She now felt ready to free herself once and for all of any remaining influence he might have, through his imagined presence, in her life.

Having developed the ability to separate or dissociate herself from overwhelmingly terrifying experiences in childhood, Ms C is now, as an adult, able to utilize this skill, together with her highly developed visual sense, to solve problems. The capacity to focus one's attention in this manner is part of a process that Erickson called "every-day trance" (Erickson & Rossi, 1976). While I do not hold with much of the theory or techniques of Ericksonian therapy, their contributions in regard to trance and their detailed attention to language has been extremely helpful to me. I therefore am alert to observe when clients indicate to me, by the manner of their presentation, that they are focused so intently on a memory that their telling of it is, so to speak, accompanied by visual and kinetic sensations. To a significant degree this applies to the therapist's frame of mind as well as to the client's. That is, when I can "see" the room that is being described, or the coffin in which Ms C is hiding herself, I assume that both of us are intently focused in on the event, which is therefore available, in an immediate sense, for therapy. I am not aware of much writing on this topic, and so must use my own rather concrete metaphors for the process described.

*Example 5:* Mr D is a man of 38 who throughout his childhood was treated with extreme violence, alternating with sexually tinged favouritism, by his mother; his father and other relatives also occasionally joined in the violence, and always condoned it. While determined never to be physically violent to his own children, he had become very distressed at the realization that he was repeating the irrational authoritarianism of his parents in his dealings with his children. In therapy our conversations increasingly focused on his childhood confusion about right and wrong, and his experience of brutality compared with his parents' presentation of themselves as just and loving.

Mr D:    "If I can generalize what I'm saying, I know all these things from when I was a child—'you mustn't do this, you mustn't do that, and so on, and so on'—and the conflict I've got is that I'm enforcing these things while in the back of my mind knowing that most of them are wrong, but I can't help myself doing it."

Therapist:    "Because, I think, somewhere in your own head that isn't clear—which is right and which is wrong. Because part of you, and maybe the adult, caring, sensitive part of you, says those rules are too strict, they're too extreme, they squash a child like they squashed me. I don't want to squash these children. I shouldn't be imposing that kind of control. But another part of you, and it's maybe the part that got it drummed into you when you were so tiny, thinks: these rules are life and death. They have to be obeyed. These are the only rules, and it feels like those two things come into conflict for you."

Mr D:    "Yes, that's the constant argument."

Therapist:    "So for example when you were a kid, would I be right in thinking you thought: Mother and Father are Mother and Father, they're in charge of everything, what they say goes."

Mr D:    "That's it."

Therapist:    "So, if you come home from school and you have a little chat with your friend, and that means you're late, that means you've been very bad, not that they're wrong to be so very strict." (This relates to an incident he had described earlier, where the family's response to his lateness had been to subject him to a species of court-martial, followed by extreme violence.)

Mr D:   "Well, I felt that I was bad—no, I felt that I didn't do that much wrong, but I still got whacked for it."

Therapist:   "How did you explain that when you were a kid?"

Mr D:   "You didn't argue back—not till later. The first time I spoke back to my mother I was 16." (This is followed by a discussion of family changes when he was 16.)

Therapist:   "Let's go back to before you were 16. Did you think that you were wrong, or did you secretly think that maybe you hadn't done anything so very terrible?"

Mr D:   "I think after I was 16 I was aware of whether I was right or wrong."

Therapist:   "But before that?"

Mr D:   "But before that I always assumed that whatever it was —I didn't really see why—but it got to be, if you got a hiding it must be for something."

Therapist:   "Even if you weren't sure what it was."

Mr D describes in detail an incident when he, at the age of four, nearly harmed his little brother of two. His mother's response to this was to throw a chair at him with such force that, although it missed him, it made a gash 6 inches long in another chair.

Therapist:   "So at the age of four, how did you make sense of the idea that for you to harm your little brother, or nearly to harm him, was wrong, but for you mother nearly to harm you was o.k.? How did you make sense of that?

Mr D:   "I don't think I've ever made sense of that, to be honest."

Therapist:   "Maybe that's because it doesn't make sense."

Mr D:   "No. If you listen to my mother now, I was such a good boy, I've been her right-hand man since I was six years old, but I can remember . . . I know that she's telling lies, and it makes me feel, I don't know, angry, or resentful."

Therapist:   "And there are bits there that just don't fit together."

Mr D:   "No."

Therapist:   "Because you're also talking, in addition to a very overstrict code—these are the absolute rules, you absolutely stick by them, if you don't stick by them you will get beaten, smacked, and so on—but you've also told me about some things that most people would describe as torture, and that must have been very hard to make sense of . . ."

Mr D:    ". . . I was terrified."

Therapist:    ". . . if you were supposed to be the bad one and she was supposed to be the good one."

Mr D:    "I was terrified, and that didn't make sense either. O.k., I did realize from a very early age that money seemed to be the biggest problem in our house. That particular occasion I told you about (relating to stealing sweets), I mean, I did it, it was a tin of sweets on the top shelf, and any one of the kids could have climbed up, because we had like a corner cupboard, like a little room, built into the house, like a shelf (this description is accompanied by vivid gestures so that the therapist is able to visualize the room clearly), and on the top shelf was this tin or jar of sweets. And you know, I know I took sweets, but they tied me to a chair. I remember they tied me to a chair in the kitchen, the gas stove was here, there was a big nail on it and it was glowing red hot, and my father had a pair of pliers—this wasn't one of them, it was both of them (i.e. both his parents were involved on this occasion)—and there's this nail, and he comes near my eye with it where you could feel it. I'm not saying they touched me with it, but the threat was there. It was in my head that they were going to do it, and they said 'Did you take those sweets?' I mean no kid in his right mind is going to say 'Yes, I did', and expect to get away with it. You see, they tell you in one breath not to tell lies, but if you've got to terrify someone they'll tell you anything, just to get out of it."

The vividness with which Mr D sets the scene, as well as his distress, tone of voice, and so on, suggest to me that while describing the events to me he is also in part reliving them. Thus there is a sense (and of course this is merely metaphor) in which he is present as the four-year-old in the room when his mother throws the chair at him, as well as as the 38-year-old in the therapy room with me, with his adult capacity to reason, and to compare his mother's responses then with his own capacity for restraint in his dealings with his children now. Thus when the adult man says that his parents' actions did not make sense, it is as if that statement retroactively clarifies some of the confusion that the terrified child has carried through into adulthood, and allows Mr D to begin to shed some of the burden of being the uncomprehending, and therefore guilty, object of so much unreasonable rage.

## 5. SEEING THE ABUSER IN CONTEXT

Therapists such as Madanes (1981, 1991) and Trepper and Barrett (1989) stress the importance of the abuser arriving at a point where he can ask for the forgiveness of the person he has abused. I agree that such an event, when sincerely meant, may make a great contribution towards the healing of all concerned. However, too many survivors experience the abuser's contrition as insincere or manipulative, and related to his desire to make a good impression on his spouse, the legal authorities, and so on. For the survivor herself, however, an important leap in her own healing process may be signalled by her understanding of the context within which the abuser's behaviour may be understood.

*Example 6:*  Ms E was a young woman who had been raped by her father; she was seen a few months later together with her mother and two adolescent sisters. The referral was made by the mother, who was deeply distressed by the consequences, for the whole family, of the rape, and the subsequent trial and sentencing of the father. Not only had the whole family suffered ostracism and discrimination within their community, but the daughters had polarized in their loyalties to different sections of the family and were on very hostile terms with one another.

Ms E had received considerable support from friends and members of the local women's refuge; from her point of view she had dealt with her own shock and distress in relation to the rape. She was now, like her mother, more concerned with the family hostilities, and felt totally unsupported and blamed within the family. For the mother and her other daughters the attempt to remain connected with, and loyal to, all family members, including the father who was now in prison, seemed impossible.

The focus of the work was on enabling the four women to find a way of supporting one another, while acknowledging that they would continue to take up different positions in relation to each other. In consequence of this work being done, Ms E arrived at the next session, with her mother and sisters, wanting to discuss her hypothesis that her father and his brother (who had also committed sexual offences in the past) had been sexually abused in childhood. A detailed discussion of his family background led on to a discussion of mother's family history, and a joint exploration between therapist and family members of the intricate ways in which patterns of abuse, of male violence and female "martyrdom", had influenced the relationships and events in their family to date. This also enabled Ms E to talk with her sisters about her determination to break the "cycle of abuse" for the future.

As said earlier, I would not push a survivor to do the kind of exploration necessary to understanding the abuser's actions in the context of his family history, circumstances, and so on. However, the participation in an exploration of the family's life, via circular questions, may well stimulate the family members to increased curiosity about the antecedents and contexts of the abuser's behaviour.

CHAPTER SIX

# The relationship
# with the "protector"

For many abuse survivors, this is often the most difficult area of therapy. Who the "protector" is seen to be will depend on the circumstances of the abuse. For example, if a child was abused by someone outside the family, both parents may have been regarded by the abused child as the people who should have protected her. Most commonly, in the cases we see, the abuser was a father or stepfather, so that from the survivor's point of view her mother is the person to whom she hoped to look for protection from abuse.

In this situation the relationship, in childhood and in adulthood, can be a very complicated one, and is usually characterized by considerable ambivalence. An abused child assumes a certain degree of omniscience and omnipotence in parents, and so assumes that her mother must know of the abuse and be able to protect her against it. When this fails to happen, the survivor may feel angry, but is unable to express or even acknowledge this, since the non-protecting parent may be the last or, indeed, the only "safe" parent she has left. It may therefore seem dangerous to confront this parent, while what feels like betrayal—because of this parent's failure to prevent the abuse—may continue to be a source of grief, anger, and incomprehension.

Like therapists, survivors will struggle with the complexities of the role of the "other" parent in abuse. Is it fair to assume that this parent should have known that abuse was taking place? Should she have been able to prevent it? What were her circumstances, which meant that she either did not notice that her child was being abused, or ignored and denied that knowledge when it came to her attention? Was she abused herself, currently or in her own childhood? What were the constraints on her freedom to act—e.g. poverty, illness, habits of dependence and service? The survivor may herself have been in a protective relationship towards her mother, whose role in the family may have been seen as one of powerlessness.

*Example 7:* Ms F, her sister Ms G, and her mother Ms H are being seen together in a second session. Ms F and Ms G were both abused by their stepfather from a young age. They have described their efforts to warn their mother against the marriage, because of the step-father's behaviour towards them. In the discussion the daughters sometimes display anger towards their mother for her continued denial of their abuse, and for her habit, in their view, of always needing to be the object of others' concern and protection. They express the view that this formed a considerable part of the neglect that they see as central to their upbringing. However, these views and emotions are expressed in ambiguous ways, frequently negated by laughter or expressions of affection and compassion for their mother; the therapist observes that the effect of the subtle communicational cues passed between them is to make the daughters dilute and even deny their sense of anger and puzzlement regarding their mother's stance on the abuse of them in childhood.

Ms F:   (She has been describing how she was able to stop her step-father's sexual abuse of her at a point when the family's circumstances altered, and she no longer regarded her mother as so vulnerable in relation to her step-father's violence) "All my life I've felt I had to look after you."

Therapist:   (to Ms H, the mother) "Any ideas why F has always felt like this?"

Mother:  "I don't know, except the fact that I was an only daughter, an only child of devoted parents, and it was quite late in life when they had me. The way my mother brought me up—I relied a lot on my mother, on my parents, you know, and this is the way they brought me up, so that I had to have my parents'—my mother's—approval for everything I did, everything I said—I had to have my mother's approval.

Ms F:  "That's how it is with me now."

Mother:  "And I couldn't really think for myself, and stand on my own two feet. I'd never done that till she died, and I was 34 then. And of course it came as a big shock then to try and stand on my own feet, which I had to learn to do. And I thought I had done it. But whether it was because F sensed this. . . ."

Ms F:  "You always talked to me so much, all your life. I knew what your life had been."

Ms H, the mother, goes on to describe a pattern in which she had relied heavily on her oldest daughter, and then when she left home at the age of 16, on the very much younger F, "to be a little mother to me". Thus from Ms F's point of view her step-father's abuse of her was happening in a context where she received many signals indicating that her mother should not be subjected to pressure. This was reinforced by the abuser's statements that if F told, her mother would have another "breakdown". Preceding the marriage to the abusing step-father Ms H (Mother) had had a "nervous breakdown" while divorcing her first husband, was agoraphobic, lost both her parents, and struggled under circumstances of severe poverty to bring up her younger children. So for Ms F being abused seemed to be the price she had to pay to keep her mother and younger sister from once again going through the terrible experiences that had preceded her mother's marriage to her step-father. Ms F's role as the "little mother" labelled her as the one who had to be responsible for protecting her mother from stress.

The burning question of the "protecting parent's" knowledge or ignorance in relation to their child's abuse is likely to form a major theme for many survivors, and can be explored in a variety of ways.

While it can be useful to start this exploration in the presence and with the participation of that parent (e.g. Ms H, above), much of the work may best be done in individual sessions. This enables the survivor, in a safe relationship with the therapist, to explore possibilities without having to be constrained by her fear of hurting that parent. It also means that she can allow herself to be angry while also holding the view that expressing that anger towards the "protecting" parent may be inappropriate or irrelevant.

*Example 8:* Ms F (previous example), during an individual session, described a vivid memory of trying, at the age of eleven, to wake her mother, who was having an afternoon nap, in order to tell her that her stepfather had been abusing her. Despite her best efforts she failed to wake her mother. This memory seemed central (and metaphorically apt) to the issues she was struggling with at that point, namely: did her mother know? and if she did not know, how was that to be explained?

The therapist suggested a task for Ms F do to in the interval between sessions. She was to clear a quiet time of several hours for herself (this meant arranging for someone to look after her two-year-old son). During this time she should think herself into the frame of mind of the eleven-year-old who was trying to wake her mother up, and to write down what she would have liked to say to her mother. Both the therapist and Ms F were fascinated by the outcome of this task, and the next two sessions were spent discussing the notes Ms F had made. She had written in the first person, in an eleven-year-old "voice", and had interspersed this with comments written, so to speak, from the meta-position of her 29-year-old observing self. She explained to the therapist that although initially she had been distressed at the thought of doing the task, she had found it interesting and clarifying. The therapist and client agreed that the latter should read out those sections that she felt were of particular significance for discussion in the session; the therapist would read the whole document later.

Ms F:  "What it showed me was amazing. I'm writing like a child, sort of pleading: "Mum, Mama, please wake up, Mum I need you, I need you', see, stuff like that. Then I was sort of apologizing, saying, 'I'm so sorry, I love you so much, Mama, and I didn't mean to hurt you like this. Oh, you will love me won't you? Hold me and tell me everything's o.k. please.' Then I've put: 'Mum, I don't want to be alone with this any more. I need you to help me—share this with me. Take this pain away' . . . and then I was crying. I remember this, this is how I was feeling at the time when I was eleven, and this is what I wanted to tell her. 'How can I tell you what it's like in my head? Oh God I'm so alone. He's hurt me badly Mum. He's hurt me. When I told you you did not listen, and you left me alone to face this. How could you not listen to me?' That was the first thing. Then I've put here : 'Your meal-ticket has sexually abused me over and over again and now I don't know how to tell you.' I called him 'your meal-ticket' because I knew she didn't love him, you see, she was looking to him for support.

The therapist and client discuss Ms F's responses to what she had written down. The format of the task enables Ms F at one and the same time to re-experience her childhood perceptions, while being able, as an adult, within the context of therapy, to comment on them from the vantage point of a more mature understanding of the events and relationships involved.

Ms F:   "I suppose now as an adult, looking back, I had nothing to be sorry for. As a child, I was sorry for doing this, and I said here 'you won't love me any more', but that's just your insecurity as a child, your confusion. As you said (cf. chapter four), children tend to blame themselves, because their adult figure is supposed to be the one who knows it all, but as a child you think you're the one who's done wrong, because they're the ones in charge. And then I felt sorry for causing my mother this pain, because I'd known what she'd been through, and then I thought 'Oh, this is going to cause you so much pain', and I blamed it on myself, which now I can see was quite ridiculous. It was the confusion between the two things—of loving her, because I've always loved her so much, and feeling sorry for what I'd done—that made me feel so bad. . . . Meal-ticket's pretty cruel, but it was a meal-ticket, my mother will admit it. I think maybe that's why I was so angry. Maybe that's the adult bit of me speaking, because as an adult I know my mother was looking for security. She didn't love him. But then I didn't understand why she married him. Maybe I felt I was paying for the meal-ticket. I suppose in my mind I was saying, this is the price for food."

As the therapy continues, Ms F's struggles with the question of her mother's knowledge or ignorance in relation to the abuse continue to be interwoven with other themes. At times it seems resolved, only to emerge again in connection with new themes.

Ms F:    "I've got to know . . . if I know, I can handle it. If she says to me . . . I thought I'd run away, when I first started thinking about this. I feared . . . I thought, well, you know, I thought no I can't. But I can handle it. If she said yes she did know, but she ran from it, I could handle it."

Therapist:    "What if she never says that, but you get clearer in your own mind what you think happened?"

Ms F:    "Maybe that would be enough, yes. Because if I knew, I'd stop asking, I'd stop feeling bitter. Because these are new feelings, that are coming out now, which have been hidden for years . . . and if I can get rid of it, I can get on a kind of adult footing that I should be on with my mother, rather than this child. I'm still this child with her, very often.

Therapist:    ". . . And the child is saying: tell me the truth, tell me what happened and make it better."

Ms F:    "I'm always trying to make her make it better. But, God, if she hasn't done it by now, I'm wasting my time . . . I don't think she can make it better. I think I've got to make it better."

There are a variety of reasons why this particular relationship may prove to be so central in the therapeutic work done by survivors. As suggested above, this may be the only relationship with an adult, in the survivor's childhood, which was non-abusive, so that it may always have felt crucial to protect this relationship against damage by criticism or uncomfortable questions. In my experience it forms an important focus for therapy where the survivor is a woman and the "protecting parent" was the mother. It is then clear that, for the survivor, thinking through her relationship with her mother has important implications for how she will live her life as an adult. For a woman to differentiate herself from her mother and to function as an autonomous adult is in any case a complex task, involving both identification and separation, as Gilligan (1987), among others, describes. When the mother is seen to have been a victim herself, helpless to protect her children, the survivor has to find a way of understanding this that will enable her to be different herself, without necessarily abandoning her relationship with her mother altogether.

*Example 9:*   Ms H (the mother in the preceding examples) has been describing, in a session attended by herself as well as her daughters Ms F and Ms G, the family's circumstances at the time of her marriage to the abusing step-father, and in particular talking about her agoraphobia. This discussion is the result of a meeting the mother and the two daughters had at home, in-between sessions, where they pooled their memories of that period, and they are now in the session presenting a view of the family pattern over time to the therapist.

Ms F:   "When we were little we knew that; I'm not saying we knew it like we know it now, but we sensed it. She was a non-person herself, right? After living with my father all those years, she was just down to a non-person. She had no confidence, nothing; but when she lost her mother, she was lost anyway, because it was the same kind of thing. When her mother told her the moon was made of cheese, the moon was made of cheese. She was totally brainwashed by Nana, so when she died when Mum was 34, Mum was nothing, she had no idea. So when that happened she was just a mess, and she had babies, right? Now she was, in my sense, the victim, the brainwashed victim, and of course as children. . . . She was trying to bring up children. She wasn't working as a person, and we were absorbing that. I mean, the first impression you have of your parent is weakness, and losing, and I think you start on a pattern for life, don't you?"

Because the survivor and her family are now beginning to look at the wider system in which the abuse occurred (cf. chapter seven), it becomes possible for the therapist to start asking questions about other aspects of the wider pattern, e.g. how men fit into this particular matrilineal system, what the implications of these insights are for the survivor's own child-rearing style, and so on. Becoming clearer about her views of her mother, as well as becoming able (or deciding) to tolerate a degree of ambiguity in the relationship, opens the door for the survivor to be a different kind of adult—one who is no longer helpless in relation to abuse, of whatever kind, and one who is able to hear her children and protect them against abuse, in a way that her own mother may have been unable to do.

It is important in considering this aspect of the work that therapists should not fall into the simplistic trap of blaming the mother of the survivor for the abuse, nor of automatically absolving her of any responsibility. If this is in the therapist's mind it will block the survivor from exploring for herself the degree to which her mother was complicit in what happened, as well as the degree to which she, too, was a victim of social and gendered patterns that make it possible for those who are powerless to be abused.

# CHAPTER SEVEN

# The wider system

## 1. FAMILY PATTERNS
### IN THE PAST, THE PRESENT, AND THE FUTURE

Unless a survivor can locate her experiences within the context of the wider systems within which she lives, she is likely to remain in a victim position, and to have certain reservations about the way in which her own behaviours may have contributed to her abuse (examples illustrating the influence of patterns in the past and the present are given in sections a and b below). A survivor may blame herself for her failure to disclose the abuse, without also thinking about the factors that constrained her behaviour, such as, for example, her mother's illness and vulnerability, the failure of the police to listen to her which meant that she was repeatedly returned home after running away, her father's depression after being made redundant, her grandfather's death, her own loneliness and desire for closeness, the family's isolation after moving house, etc., etc. It is therefore crucial that this contextualizing work should be done, but it is unlikely that it can be done fully until the survivor has dealt to some degree with the issues described in chapters five and six. While her thinking and behaviour within relationships get organized by guilt, self-blame, and "family secrets", she will find it difficult to begin to consider the other ways in which her life is patterned by styles of interaction learned within an abusing system.

This is where working from a systemic base can contribute significantly to work with adult survivors. Individually focused work with a survivor, which considers only her experience of abuse, the impact of this on her feelings about herself, her sexuality, and her ability to handle intimate relationships, while it is very important, does not in my view go far enough. It is enlightening and liberating for the survivor to consider how the abuse she suffered was located within the family system at the time, as well as to consider the many ways in which her behaviour and relationships have been patterned by the abuse. It is this that enables her to make the changes that alter the way she interacts with others who are significant to her in the present and the future.

### a. Identifying patterns from the past

*Example 10:*   Mr and Ms I (both in their thirties at the time of therapy) had both been sexually abused as children, he by his father and, he thought, by his mother, and she by her brother. Mr I told of a frightening childhood in which his father frequently came home drunk, and indiscriminately raped and beat his mother as well as the children. His mother would sometimes take refuge in his bed, and this was when he thought she might have sexually abused him. Because this took the form of cuddling and a mutual search for comfort, and because he pitied her, he had been left with considerable confusion about the nature of what had happened between him and his mother, about his own feelings, and about how to interpret this relationship (compare with Example 2, in chapter five). He veered between rage and pity, whereas his attitude towards his father seemed less ambiguous. He left home to marry Ms I, whom he had known since childhood, when they were both about seventeen. In the years since their marriage he had found himself behaving increasingly violently, and in other ways abusively, towards his wife. It was when he saw their young child beginning to be involved in the marital rows that he sought out therapy. At this point he was appalled at the similarity between his own actions and those of his father, and said: "I realized I'd decided it was a choice between being a bastard and a victim, and I was not going to be a victim."

Ms I's older brother had sexually abused her from early childhood. When she was eleven he attempted full intercourse, and at this point she was able to invoke the help of older siblings to stop him. In her view her family, and her mother's family of origin, operated to rules that said "men are the only ones that count". The family ethos was such that she had concluded there was no chance of being believed or supported by the adults, if it was a question of her word against her brother's. She had formed the view that "this is a woman's life. There's no use expecting more." She had therefore also "put up" with her husband's abusive behaviour towards her. It was only when her husband sought out therapy for himself that she had begun to hope that perhaps for both of them there might be different options; significantly this meant for both wife and husband that they might offer their children a better childhood and future than they themselves had had.

Any or all of the survival tactics adopted by children can become handicaps to them as they grow into adulthood. Mr I resorted to "identification with the aggressor"; Ms I to stoicism; some people put a protective layer of fat, or cheerfulness, or invisibility around themselves. Many will continue to believe that they are worth nothing; their actions of self-abnegation or self-harm may be seen by others as an invitation to abuse them further.

Readers will have noted in chapter six that the clients quoted were no longer talking only—or even at all—about the abuse, but were talking about the pattern of relationships within which it was possible for the children to experience themselves as neglected and unprotected, or prematurely burdened with adult responsibility. That is, they were looking to alter not only the immediate perceived effects of being abused on an individual member of the family, but were considering the nature of their relationships, and ways to alter these that might lead to greater self-actualization for all family members.

A child's experiences within the family system in which she has been abused will require her to learn certain patterns of behaviour and meaning that may continue to influence her views of herself and her interactions with others. However, she will not be the only one in the family affected in a manner detrimental to her development of her own potential. Talking of "the family" can obscure individual differences—in power, in desires, in commitment—but equally there is a risk in assuming that the "victim" is the only one affected within a family in which abuse has occurred.

The therapist's curiosity (Cecchin, 1987), expressed via circular, open-minded questions about the patterning of events and relationships, is likely also to stimulate the curiosity of family members about their own experiences. "What else was going on in the wider family circle at the time? " "When A was doing this, what was B doing?" "What births, deaths, losses, stresses were occurring simultaneously?" "What is your explanation for this?" "Why was this child abused rather than that one?" "How do you explain this—otherwise loving—father's blindness to his child's suffering?" "How did this mother decide to remain with an abusing man, at the cost of her children's welfare?" "How can we fit these pieces together and arrive at an explanation that offers an acceptable meaning, and opens a door to the future?"

*Example 11:* Ms E and her family (discussed in Example 6) looked at the way in which family patterns and individual differences had combined to lead up to the crisis of her rape by her father and his subsequent imprisonment. In the first session there had been some discussion of the history of violence between Ms E and her father; the consensus of opinion was that if one of them had murdered the other, no-one would have been very surprised. Mother and Ms E's sisters were surprised that the relationship had culminated in rape, and searched for explanations of this. For Ms E herself, however, the rape was a further step in the escalation of violence. She saw it less as a sexual act than as an assertion of dominance (cf. note 4).

At the beginning of the second session Ms E said she had been asking some questions, of herself, her mother, and her father's mother. Her father's brother had been in trouble previously for exposing himself. "I've been wondering why two brothers—

the only children—should both do something like this. I was wondering if anything had happened to them when they were younger." She describes how her father was born following his mother being raped at the age of fourteen. "Can hatred be passed on in the genes?" Her paternal grandfather (whom she never knew) has been described to her as a very violent man, and she goes on to speculate: "Maybe that grandfather (father's father) also abused my father and his brother."

Ms E then turns to her mother:

Ms E: "Will you permit me to bring this up? How do you feel about your father?"

Mother: "I don't know if it's just luck or what—but my father exposed himself as well. I got to know about it when I was eleven. He never touched any of us children. He did it in the house when people called, but not to us."

Ms E: "So how do you feel about him? Do you hate him?"

Mother: "No, I don't hate him. He never did anything to us. As I understood it as a child it was a sickness, because he was put into a mental hospital."

Ms E expresses the view that her father also needed help, and blames her mother for having done nothing about it. "It seems to me he had things on his mind for a long time—sick things. It seems like this sort of thing had been building up for a long time, and I was the result. He needed help a long time ago. I can't see why my mother hadn't noticed."

Ms E's mother goes on to talk about her own family patterns. Because her mother was preoccupied with her father's problems and frequent hospitalizations, it fell to her, as oldest daughter of six children, to stand in for her mother. In her view this amplified her version of her family's placating style, so that she saw herself as primarily there to look after others, no matter what, to try to keep the peace, and to see all points of view. She describes her husband as someone always prone to violence, and Ms E, her oldest daughter, as being just like her father and her father's side of the family: "They all have a temper. When they lose their temper they straight away want to act—with their hands." The family discuss the way in which Ms E, in particular, has been seen in the family as the only one who could stand up to her father; this often took the form of attempting to protect her mother. The other daughters would tend to withdraw and avoid the father's anger, but Ms E "has always fought back as far as I can remember. She would stand there and defy him."

Ms E: "I used to stand up for myself and have an answer—it wasn't cheeky as I thought, but to state an opinion. It would turn into an argument with my father, and I always got the worst end of it, no matter what."

Mother and daughter go on to describe the way in which each of them would "get in the way" to block violence against the other. In response to repeated questions from Ms E as to why her mother did nothing to get help, or put an end to the continued violence, her mother says: "Years ago, when the children were smaller, I used to think, shall I ask somebody to come in from outside? But then I was afraid, because of not knowing about places like these (e.g. the F.I.). I was afraid if I called someone they'd take my children away, and that frightened me. So I did the best I could on my own; if the quarrel got to a violent stage I used to get in the middle. I didn't mind—I'd save my girls a lot of violence."

By considering the way that family patterns have built up over time, the way in which the styles of functioning, which partners bring from their families of origin, make a "fit" in the new family, which can then in turn lead to a further escalation of a pernicious pattern, the family members begin to find some answers to their questions regarding *why* abuse happened, to *whom*, and *when*. Perhaps more importantly, it enables them to begin to think of ways that these patterns can be changed (cf. section b below). Understanding more about the past does not mean that participants are invited to feel overwhelmed by guilt at their part in the events; rather, that recognizing the pattern means it can be changed. Looking at the systemic consequences of actions taken—perhaps in good faith, perhaps because no alternative seemed viable—enables people to begin to strive for different actions, and thus different consequences in the future. It may also lead to a re-evaluation of relationships and blaming. Ms E's realization that her mother did see the violence, and hearing her mother's reasons for not taking more decisive action, make a difference to her, even though she does not agree with her mother's reasoning. The realization, for both of them, that they were often similarly motivated by an intention to draw the violence onto themselves, in order to protect the other, makes a bond between them. The discussion about the father's background, while not altering his responsibility for raping his daughter, does give all the family members a frame into which to place this previously incomprehensible act. In consequence Ms E's mother arranges to talk with her husband and his probation officer, and starts to plan for therapy for herself and her husband, when he will be released from prison, as a condition for the continuation of their relationship. This makes it more possible for Ms E to accept her mother's intention to stand by her husband *and* her daughter—whereas this had previously been seen as a stark choice of losing either her daughter or her husband—and to negotiate conditions that will make it possible for Ms E to retain contact with her mother and her sisters without having to see her father again.

### b. Identifying patterns in the present

As therapy continues, the focus of the client–therapist discussion will shift from the traumas of the past to relationships in the present. A survivor begins to evaluate her way of "being-in-the-world", and the kinds of typical relationships in which she may find herself repeatedly playing the same parts. When she understands how these patterns may have been set up in the past, it may also be possible for her to recognize that they no longer serve a useful purpose. Thus she can begin to break the habits that have kept her enmeshed in abusive relationships.

These abusive relationships may vary right across the board from continuations of sexual abuse initiated in childhood to the sort of every-day abuse suffered by unassertive people, and which may not previously have been labelled as such. Two brief examples will illustrate the opposite ends of this spectrum:

*Example 12a:* Ms J (cf. note 5) had suffered multiple abuse from several family members in childhood. From the age of twelve she had also been abused by the much older son of a close friend of her parents', who knew that she had been abused previously and considered her "fair game". She subsequently married him, as a result of considerable family pressure and her own belief that no-one else would have her; she was still married to him, and they had three children whom she loved in an anxious and protective way, and who treated her (like their father did) as the family skivvy.

For Ms J to begin to untangle the threads of her own attitudes and self-valuation, together with the habits of relationship as perceived by the others in her family, was—understandably—a mammoth task. To become less of a doormat to her sons and daughter she had to demonstrate in the family that she considered herself worthy of respect. In order to do this she had to make changes within her marital relationship; this was difficult for her, not only because she was literally trying to alter a lifetime's assumptions and "rules" between herself and her husband, but also because he was by now old, frail, and very dependent upon her. Before she could attempt to bring about these changes, she had to struggle with her own self-doubt and self-hatred; as someone whose entire life to date had been defined within the context of abuse, it was not easy to begin to assert her own entitlement not to be abused. It is a tribute to her that, despite these terrible circumstances, she was able to achieve a measure of autonomy.

*Example 12b:*   Ms K began to look at many of her current relationships through the lens of her knowledge of patterns of abuse. She noticed that she was abused in many different ways, from having her bottom pinched, to being put down or patronized in discussion, to being taken for granted, to having her family and friends take advantage of her willingness to be of service. She noticed that she responded to all these situations with a ready smile and an inability to say no or to present her own views and desires in a way likely to be heard. By calling these situations abusive she found the courage to act more assertively when they occurred; the feedback, much to her delight, was positive, rather than the rejection she had feared. Building on this, she began to be firmer with her young child, who had acquired a reputation as a tantrum-throwing monster who was not wanted in nursery school or in other children's homes. She realized that she had been over-indulgent with her child because she could not believe that he would ever love her, since she had considered herself unworthy of anyone's love or esteem. As her self-confidence grew, she also said no appropriately to her son.

In families where abuse has occurred, the family members may cling closely together and fear separation. This pattern of family closeness may be seen as predating the occurrence of abuse, and/ or as following on as a consequence of the abuse. However this sequence is punctuated, abuse survivors and their families may struggle to untangle their interdependence so as to allow a degree of autonomy and differentiation between themselves. At a later stage in therapy, then, experimenting with closeness and distance may be useful to enable family members to make up their (different) minds about what feels comfortable and desirable to them.

*Example 13*:   Ms L and Ms M were sisters who had both been abused, and who had formed each other's main support throughout childhood and adulthood; although both had married, it was clear to all participants that the sisterly relationship took priority over all others. They both saw the struggle for greater autonomy as essential, partly in order to achieve their own liberation from the effects of their childhood abuse, and partly in order that their adult lives should be able to be open to other relationships (e.g. with their spouses) and individual goals and interests. However, both were very afraid of the unknown, potentially catastrophic, consequences of separation. As Ms L said: "We can't be sure, if we get more separate, that we might not discover that we really hate each other."

The therapist suggested a "homework" task that they could do whenever the opportunity arose. If one sister acted in a way that was judged appropriately "distancing" by the other, she should be rewarded by an act of "sisterly closeness". For example, they reported that Ms L had reached into Ms M's handbag, taken out a letter addressed to Ms M (by another sister), and read it. Ms M objected to this, saying: "That's my handbag and my letter, and you're not to go into it like that without asking me." After being initially taken aback, Ms L recognized this as an appropriate boundary-setting action and rewarded Ms M by taking her out for tea. In this way separateness does not have to mean abandonment or hatred, and closeness does not have to mean mutual engulfment.

Survivors may also struggle with the idea that, on the one hand, they are damaged, and no one worth while will want to be close to them, or, on the other hand, that anyone who seeks to be close to them must be strange by definition. "You're scared of being happy, that things might go wrong. And then you think, what's wrong with the guy—he must have a screw loose. But after all's said and done, I'm an O.K. person, and I think to myself, it's my turn to be happy now."

### c. "Positive negatives"

It may be difficult for a survivor to change patterns of interaction in the present or the future when these are connected with behaviours that have been labelled or experienced as positive. Examples might include being special, seeming to hold power in the family (e.g. to prevent its break-up), sharing adult secrets, receiving some sort of caring or physical pleasure; these will be discussed in more detail below. These so-called positives will have a paradoxical status and may therefore be difficult to disentangle and to shift. They are likely to form part of the attitudes and actions the survivor adopted in order to survive, so that letting go of them will seem to threaten survival itself.

### Approval and "being special"

It may seem to a child that being chosen to be abused signifies that they occupy a special place in the family. There is not much external evidence for this (La Fontaine, 1990). Research suggests that which child is abused has more to do with opportunity, family structure, and circumstances than with any special interest in or fondness for this particular child. However, the abused child may be told by the abuser that she is special; in addition, a child who is in all other respects neglected may value the attention she receives from the abuser, even though its price is so high. She is therefore in the position of being a "good child" in the eyes of the abuser, through being a "bad child" in her own eyes, and in her anticipation of the way in which she might be blamed for the abuse if it ever came to light. Survivors frequently tell of the confusion they felt as to the "goodness" or "badness" of what was happening, even in the eyes of the abuser. This may be compounded by the abuser talking to them in ambiguous terms, e.g. praising them for their compliance, while reviling them and holding them responsible for his "seduction". Such a child may then live in fear of the abuser "telling on them".

A child who is being abused will have learned that her own wishes are insignificant compared with those of others. Her general behaviour in the family and outside it may be highly compliant, and she may receive praise for this. If this is the only aspect of her behaviour that is ever valued, it will continue to be hard for her to risk disapproval by standing up for herself.

*Example 14:*   Ms N had been sexually abused from early childhood by her father, her mother, and her grandmother. Her father was the pimp who managed her mother's and grandmother's work as prostitutes. Ms N had always been seen, within and outside the family, as a quiet, compliant child. She was a model pupil at school, and it appeared, in retrospect, that she had kept a very clear boundary between her bizarre home life and her school life, where she was seen as a high-achieving model pupil. Her abuse came to attention when her parents complained to their local social services that she was out of their control. The occasion for this was that, at the age of fifteen, she had wanted to attend a Christian youth meeting at school in the evening with a friend, and had wanted to wear make-up.

*Secrets and power*

Children feel their exclusion from the world of adult secrets—which includes sexuality—keenly, and will glory in the importance that comes from being asked to share a secret with a grown-up (think, for example, of the thrill that accompanies secret preparations, with one parent, for the other parent's birthday surprise). The negative experience of being used for an adult's sexual pleasure may therefore become confusingly looped in with the pleasure and sense of power that derives from holding a secret. In addition to making the child feel important, possession of secret knowledge may also be seen as a weapon against other adults, where the child's relationship with them is based on neglect, exclusion, or blame.

A child who is being sexually abused may also be in the role of protecting the non-abusing parent (cf. chapter six) against intolerable stress, and of keeping the family together. Children are frequently told by the abuser that if they tell, it will have dire effects: mother will die or have a nervous breakdown, the abuser will go to gaol and this will be the child's fault, their siblings will be put in care, and the family will break up. While this sort of responsibility is inappropriate and false, a child may derive a sense of importance from it that goes some way towards placing a positive value on their sufferings. Our culture values altruism and sacrifice for the sake of others; it is not surprising to hear, then, that children attempt to make some positive meaning for themselves out of the experience of being the family's "saviour" or "scapegoat". This can then become a difficult role to give up, particularly when the survivor is not yet sure that they have any other value for those around them.

*Example 15:*   Mr D (Example 5) as the oldest child in his family, the one who took the brunt of the abuse, and the one who was labelled as his mother's favourite, continued to be seen as "Mr Fix-it" by all his family members. He was the one who was always available to sort out everyone's difficulties, who laid down the law throughout his extended family regarding what was permitted and what was not. His extremely tight control of his children's behaviour, long after an age when this might have been regarded as appropriate, had been creating considerable family tension. His wife complained about the degree of intrusion she experienced, in their life as a couple, from constant demands by his and her wider family for assistance, arbitration, and rescue. Mr D himself was tired of his centrality, but feared that without this he would fade from the family's consciousness. He could not see that anyone might have any reason for being with him, except in so far as he was able to be of service. It seemed to him that if he let go of the reins controlling his family's actions, they would all immediately escape from him. Therapy sessions with a variety of members of Mr D's current family as well as the wider clan made it possible to begin to explore different options for connection amongst all of them; Mr D began to hope that by shedding power and control he might gain some faith in the disinterestedness of the attachment his relations felt for him.

## Victim status

Being a victim may, in childhood, seem the only identity open to an abused child. As time goes on, the role of victim may take on the flavour of a "career", or an addiction. This will be influenced by cultural, as well as psychological factors. In most cultures there is a considerable iconography that makes the role of martyr seem an attractive and praiseworthy one. A child who finds herself in such a role may feel unable, as time goes by, to let go and experiment with other ways of construing herself in relation to her world. Remaining stuck in the position of victim may be connected with issues of approval and power (cf. the subsections above), as well as with vengeance.

> *Example 16:* Ms O saw her extreme obesity partly as a way of keeping herself sexually invisible, and partly as a sort of self-destructive vengeance on her abuser. Her childhood experience was such that the abuse had been labelled as love, and accompanied by lavish gifts of sweets. "Every time I stuff myself with chocolate I say to him: 'See what your 'love' is doing to me? It's killing me.' She talked of herself as being addicted to the role of victim: "It's like being drunk. Nothing else will ever be as exciting."

This is the excitement that comes from self-destructive behaviour, and the seeking out of danger, which is experienced as having the urgency of compulsion. It may be characterized by the kinds of self-mutilation or risk-taking by which survivors sometimes express their distress and sense of damage. However, it is important not to overlook the difficult truth voiced by Ms O above—that there may be a kind of intoxication about living on the edge, which makes ordinary non-victim daily life seem dull and tame.

### Timing

The timing and style of dealing with the issues gathered together here under the title of "positive negatives" will obviously be crucial. While the survivor remains attached to these old styles of interacting she will find it difficult to move on into relationships where she will not be abused. However, it is important that, in the process of examining the apparent benefits that accrued from her position as the abused child, this should not lead her again to feeling responsible for being abused. In dealing with these areas, therefore, both therapist and client must repeatedly link them with the issues discussed in the rest of part two.

### d. Changing patterns in the future

By asking hypothetical questions about the future (Selvini et al., 1980; Penn, 1985), the therapist enables clients to consider the consequences of changing or not changing. When individuals are afraid to move, feel unable to shift patterns of interaction that they do not like, and seem obliged to live with the devil they know rather than the unknown, it can be useful to explore a variety of hypothetical futures, without at this stage having to make a firm commitment to any of these options. An individual may be holding back from change because they feel, for the time being, unable to see the way forward; on the other hand, they may fear that further change will cost too much in regard to current relationships that they value. The positive systemic connotation of family patterns, which is so closely associated with the work of the Milan therapists (Selvini et al., 1978), is significantly associated with an appreciation on the part of the therapist that much may be lost in the status quo if change is pursued blindly for its own sake.

In addition, letting go of the past may mean letting go of past relationships, or of the hope for reparation. When a client explores hypothetical questions around the idea of, for example, no longer being organized by concepts of guilt and sacrifice in her relation-ships, she may have to confront the possibility that some of those to whom she has been close would not like her or find her quite as amenable as they had done in the past. By considering these issues she is in a position to make more informed choices.

Having come to a clear view of her own history, having looked critically at her own actions and those of the significant others, and having defined herself as a survivor, not a victim, she is also now in a position to make a difference to the future for herself and those in whose lives she will play a significant part. Perhaps one can only say that a survivor has overcome the effects of being abused when she becomes able to deal differently with new, potentially abusive situations, and when she can provide her children (if she has any) with a different family atmosphere from the one in which she grew up.

*Example 17:* In the course of therapy Ms P had made many changes in her views of herself and her relationships with others. Before coming to therapy she had spent several years on anti-depressant medication after the birth of her child and the break-up of her marriage. She had been regarded by her family at one and the same time as the one who would always be available to help them out and support them when troubles came, and also as a hopeless failure who would never amount to anything in her own right; this continued the family patterns in which she had been sexually abused. Individually and in family sessions she had worked to free herself of the internalized and interactional patterns of the past, so that she now felt able to meet the world with assertiveness and self-confidence based on her changed self-perception as well as on daily feedback from her new actions and relationships. So, for example, she had resumed an educa-tion that had been severely disrupted by the effects of sexual abuse (e.g. emotional preoccupation and fear interfering with her concentration on school work, as well as being kept at home often in order to keep her stepfather company). She had found work which enabled her to create better living conditions for herself and her young son, was writing poetry, had made new friends with whom she did not play the "martyr" role that had previously been habitual with her, and had established new relationships with her family that better satisfied her desire to be lovingly connected with them as well as autonomous.

At this point in the therapy she had met a man with whom she felt she might become involved in a more serious and lasting relationship than had seemed possible before. This renewed some anxieties about her own judgement and ability to trust men, in relation to her fear that he might abuse her or her son. By looking at what she had learned from her own history that would make it possible for her to be different now she felt reconnected with her own strengths. For example, the fact that when she was small her mother did not listen to her when she told her about being abused by her stepfather made it *more* likely that she herself would now listen to and believe her son if he should need to report such abuse to her. Because of her own experience she had already taught her son to speak out, to say no, and to be clear about what sort of touching he liked and did not like. It was possible for her to distinguish with more confidence between fears based on the past and realistic uncertainties in the present and the future, as she listened to her answers to a series of hypothetical questions, e.g. "Suppose you were wrong to trust X and he did try to abuse your son, what would be the first sign for you that things were not right?" "How could you protect your son while getting to know X better?" "What have you learned that will help you trust your judgement about men?" "How are you different now from how your mother was then?" "What is different about your relationship with your son that will make it possible for you to believe him if he did want to tell you about things that were upsetting him?"

In a sense Ms P could be said to arrive at the same position that all parents have to occupy in these days of increased awareness of the risks of abuse, namely to know that these risks exist, and to do all in their power to minimize risks and keep communication open; that is, she no longer felt that her own experience of being abused would place her child in a victim role.

She then went on to consider her own fears in relation to the new man in her life. Initially it seemed to her that she could only trust him if she had an ironclad guarantee as to his probity, and as to the certainty that the relationship would last forever. Again hypothetical questions allowed her to explore her possible reactions to a variety of contingencies, e.g. if she found that he was wanting to behave abusively towards her, or if the relationship was to turn out to be rewarding but not permanent. At the end of therapy Ms P concluded with a kind of survey of life's pleasures and uncertainties, as she had experienced them to date, and as she anticipated the future might hold for her. She felt able to continue to meet life with a more open stance, and without the sort of tight control over all eventualities which she had attempted to exercise in the past. After all, she said, with a powerful laugh, "I'm a survivor. I shall keep reminding myself of that."

## 2. SOCIO-CULTURAL PATTERNS IN THE PAST, THE PRESENT, AND THE FUTURE

As well as locating her experience of abuse within her family patterns, it is also useful for a survivor to locate these within the wider cultural patterns of her society. (Readers are referred to chapter two for an extended discussion of this issue.) When a therapist is willing to talk with a client, on the basis of the client's actual experiences, about the way in which men and women are socialized in her society, about that society's views concerning the different views that are held about the exercise of power between men and women, and adults and children, and the general idealization of "the family", then it becomes possible for the abuse survivor to locate her experience within a context that does not merely indict her particular family. As long as abuse remains closeted within the family, in the way that professionals talk about it with each other and with clients, then individual family members, including the survivor herself, will be expected to carry the shame of the abuse. Counsellors working with survivors of torture (Buus & Agger, 1988; Blackwell, 1990) make it clear that it is essential for such a survivor to contextualize their experience within the political ideology held by themselves and their torturer; thus the torture is not merely an event between a victim and a sadistic deviant—it is placed within the cultural and ideological context that makes it possible.

A walk to the reader's nearest corner shop will illustrate this point. The top shelves of the magazine rack will be filled with explicit pictures of women in postures demonstrating vulnerability and passivity to the gaze of the observer (and this gaze is by definition male; cf. Berger, 1972). A slightly more intensive scrutiny will show that many of these women are depicted in postures, styles, or clothing that imply that they are very young. The same observations can be made in fashion magazines. The message received by observers—and these observers are likely to include would-be abusers as well as children—is that sexual relationships in which imbalances of power are considered erotic are within the norms of our culture. A further look along the shelves will take this argument another step further, to the apparent acceptability of violence, bondage, and fear as accompaniments of erotic excitement. The example of the neighbourhood shop is perhaps very literal, but it is intended to illustrate the point that we receive many cultural messages, of which we are often only subliminally aware, that place the sexual abuse of children within, not outside, cultural definitions of what is tolerated.

In considering these issues with clients, the therapist of course needs to be careful not to push her own values and political convictions down the client's throat. To do so would be abusive and non-therapeutic. However, a sensitive therapist will find many openings that will make it possible to link the individual survivor's experience to that of others who have undergone the same experience, and to the cultural context in which the survivor lives. Not to do this is as much a breach of therapeutic responsibility as is the insensitive thumping of the therapist's own particular soap-box. At a point when the survivor herself begins to express interest in knowing that she is not alone in having been abused in childhood—and this knowledge is increasingly available via the media—she might value reading about the experiences of others. I will sometimes lend clients books or recommend reading that can be obtained from the public library (e.g. Bass & Thornton, 1983).

Clarity about the familial and the socio-cultural context in which she has been abused enables the survivor to get a clearer perspective on the experiences in the past of herself and her family, and also to be clearer about the future directions she wants to pursue, for herself and those close to her.

# PART THREE

# SOME QUESTIONS AND DILEMMAS

To repeat what was said at the beginning of this book, the guidelines discussed in the preceding pages do not pretend to be a blueprint, nor to be the only way to work with abuse survivors. Individual, group, or family work with survivors, based on different theoretical orientations from the systemic approach discussed here, have all proved helpful. I hope to have given workers who are not familiar with a family/systemic approach some ideas which may chime with their own experience, and which may be capable of integration into their own models; similarly I hope that family therapists will be encouraged to consider that useful work may be done with the whole systems, past and current, within which the survivor lives, even though only the survivor herself may be available for therapy. Before going on to consider in chapter nine some of the questions that face workers and survivors, I will discuss, in chapter eight, two types of dilemma: personal implications for therapists, and therapeutic pitfalls.

# PART TWO

# SOME QUESTIONS
# AND DILEMMAS

# Dilemmas

## 1. PERSONAL IMPLICATIONS FOR THERAPISTS

Most therapists who work with survivors agree that the stress for therapists may be greater than in many other areas of work. There are presumably numerous reasons for this, but I shall refer briefly to only a few of these.

Given the high incidence of sexual abuse, it is quite likely that some therapists will themselves be abuse survivors. This is made more likely by the fact—generally acknowledged—that those of us who choose to go into the helping professions do not do so only for reasons of altruism, but are often motivated by the desire to understand or solve some of our own and our families' problems. Working with sexual abuse can therefore trigger memories of abuse for therapists; these memories may refer to facts previously known, or may be brought into awareness for the first time, e.g. in the form of "flashbacks" in response to material discussed by clients. If a therapist is herself an abuse survivor this is no reason not to work with survivors; indeed, she may well bring an increased depth of understanding to her work, *provided* firstly that she can be sure that she has previously, in some other forum, dealt with the effects of her own abuse, and secondly provided that she has the opportunity to examine and talk through the current effects of clients' revelations on her own state of mind. This support is crucial if she is to avoid imposing her own preoccupations or distress on clients; supportive opportunities to look at her practice and her own responses may be provided by colleagues, supervisors, friends, or partners.

Even if the therapist is not an abuse survivor herself, the material discussed by clients may make her feel shaken. So much of what abuse survivors have to say relates to the abuses of power in our society, and to the complexities and imbalances in relationships between the genders. We cannot, therefore, expect to stand aloof from this material. Our own gender identity, our relationships with partners, children, and parents, and our cherished fantasies about childhood are all likely to be subjected to new scrutiny in consequence of working with abuse survivors. This may be painful, and may at times make the therapist feel excessively vulnerable; however, if we believe that change in an interactive system is likely to affect all its members, we should not, as therapists, wish to remain untouched by the changes that our clients are exploring.

While, in my view, working with the support of colleagues is crucial in this kind of work, it should also be recognized that team relationships will become strained at times, precisely because all involved will be feeling stressed and disturbed by the nature of the work. We only have to look at the almost unprecedented polarization of opinions stirred up by discussions of sexual abuse to realize that there is no reason why working teams should be immune from such dissent. Being able to deal with this as a colleague group is likely to add immeasurably to the capacity of individual therapists to work well, and to seek consultation when appropriate.

## 2. COMMON PITFALLS

The contemplation of errors in therapy can be useful: other people's errors make us feel better about our own, and our own errors may help us to deal differently in the future. There is a sense in which it could be said that if we never made any errors, we would never learn anything. In addition to the problems discussed in chapter three, where the therapist's distress makes it difficult for clients to give a full account of what happened to them, there are a number of other pitfalls which seem to me to occur commonly, and which I shall mention briefly:

*Example 18*:   A talented and intelligent young woman of seventeen had been sexually abused since early childhood by her parents and other members of the family. Her parents seemed so revolting to myself and my colleagues that we entertained not a moment's doubt about her desire to be separated from them. We accordingly swept into a multitude of plans for her future, which particularly betrayed our assumption that she would of course go to university (like us), would attain a nice middle-class life (like us), and would never wish to see her parents again (like us). It took a serious suicide attempt on her part before we were able to hear what her own very different goals were.

It is to be hoped that therapists will not often make errors like the one above. Nevertheless, it is easy to make the same type of error in a less obvious way:

*Example 19:*   Ms Q had been seen for the first few sessions together with members of her family, with whom she was in daily contact. The whole family, and particularly she and her mother, talked everything over with each other. In the view of myself and my colleague this undifferentiated pattern was significant in the history of her abuse. When I subsequently saw her for some individual sessions I decided to suggest to her that she might find it useful to give herself permission not to discuss what happened in individual sessions with her family. At the time I saw this as the beginning of her exploration of her own autonomy. However, it produced much stress throughout the family. In retrospect my colleague and I realized that, firstly, we had mis-timed this suggestion—at a later stage the family members, including Ms Q, started of their own volition to explore the possibilities and risks of more separateness; and, secondly, that in suggesting to Ms Q that what happened in the therapy might be kept secret I had replicated the abuse situation, in which her stepfather had instructed her not to tell her mother what happened between them.

Since it is not unusual for several children in one family to be abused, therapists may face requests from several siblings for individual therapy (cf. also Hall & Lloyd, 1989, for a discussion on this topic). In family therapy this situation will not often crop up, since the whole family will be seen together. However, it is our practice, when working with abuse survivors, to see them for some individual sessions even where other family members may be available. This is because there are areas, particularly to do with sexuality, details of abuse, flashbacks, and so on, where the survivor is entitled to, and is likely to make good use of, the privacy of an individual session in order to explore these matters to her satisfaction. This may, however, then lead to difficulties if the therapist does not think clearly enough about the potential pitfalls, or feels caught up in the obligation to be available whenever she is asked.

*Example 20*:   Ms R's sister, Ms T, had made extremely good use of therapy sessions with me, and was now coming to the end of the work. Ms R had attended family sessions, which had been interspersed amongst Ms T's individual sessions. Ms R now said that she herself was ready to do some individual work on her own history of abuse—something she had been unwilling to think about until then. She insisted that she had to see me.

Although I was very aware of the potential pitfalls, and discussed them with Ms R and with my colleagues, I nevertheless agreed. The dilemma was as follows: Ms R was the younger sister, and saw herself as always having lived in the shadow of Ms T, who was mother's favourite and confidante. She felt that she always came second; indeed, the fact that Ms T had borne the brunt of the sexual abuse by their father was, at times, seen by Ms R as yet another proof that she was second-best: "I wasn't even good enough to abuse." She then also despised herself for having such feelings. From her point of view seeing any other therapist would be construed as second-best, since her sister had benefited from seeing me. On the other hand, being seen by me in therapy *after* her sister also constituted second-best, and made her fear that I would be comparing her progress or lack of progress detrimentally with that of her sister.

Despite our awareness of the difficulties implicit in agreeing to this structure for therapy, and frequent discussion between myself and Ms R about them, I did not succeed in helping her, so that the decision to see someone else had to be made at a later stage, when it was presumably more painful. If faced with such a decision again, I hope I would say no firmly, despite my fear that refusing to see Ms R would be interpreted by her as a confirmation that I really preferred her sister.

The dilemmas posed above relate not only to aspects of technique, but to the therapist's own emotions and patterns of behaviour becoming caught up in therapeutic decisions (in other words to issues which in psychodynamic therapies would be described as dealing with problems of transference and countertransference).

*CHAPTER NINE*

# Questions

## 1. IS SEXUAL ABUSE ALWAYS HARMFUL?

This is a very difficult question, one that gets asked repeatedly and stirs up considerable emotion in all who attempt to discuss it. As clinicians and researchers, most of our knowledge about the longer-term effects of sexual abuse comes from the testimony of people who have sought out help—that is, from people who do consider themselves to have been affected significantly and adversely. It is very hard then to know or guess whether there are significant numbers of survivors who do not seek out professional help, and who do not need it. While the figures and their reliability are discussed in some detail in most of the literature on this topic, my own conclusion has to be that we do not, at present, know. For widely differing views on this contentious topic, see, for example, La Fontaine (1990) (valuable not only for her clarity and judiciousness, but also because she looks at U.K. and American figures, which most other writers do not do), Furniss (1991), Haugaard and Repucci (1988), and Frude (1985, and in press).

In addition there is a problem about some of the definitions of the long-term adverse effects of sexual abuse, in the case of women.

There is general agreement, among those professionals who work with adult survivors, that the effects of abuse might show themselves in the form of low self-esteem, lack of assertiveness, depression, and problems in sexual and maternal relationships. However, when we look at the research done on the socialization of women, and the norms set for female behaviour (in Western culture), we find that many of the behaviours and "traits" that would be seen to characterize "neurotic" women, such as those listed above, would also be used to prescribe sex-role-appropriate behaviour in women (e.g. Penfold & Walker, 1984). If significant numbers of "ordinary" women are depressed, lack self-esteem and assertiveness, are unhappy in their sex lives, and have problems of confidence and enjoyment in rearing their children, are we to conclude that all these women have been sexually abused, or that sexually abused women do not have problems that are different in kind from those of other women, though they might be more severe? Or should we begin to ask ourselves whether the majority of women are showing the symptoms of growing up in a culture based on inequities in power in which they find themselves, as females, at the bottom of the hierarchy?

## 2. WHY IS SEXUAL ABUSE BEING DISCLOSED MORE FREQUENTLY NOW?

Sexual abuse is not new, nor is some level of acknowledgement of its existence (La Fontaine, 1990). Nevertheless, the recent awareness of it, and the public attention paid to it, has overwhelmed professionals and public alike with a realization of its prevalence in our society. McCarthy and Byrne (1988), discussing sexual abuse in an Irish context, hypothesize that sexual abuse may be occurring more frequently as a symptom of the breakdown of the nuclear family in an age when marital separation and women's independence are on the increase. While we cannot be certain, at this stage, whether sexual abuse is occurring more often, or being disclosed more often, my own view would differ from theirs.

I would assume, given the information we have about the prevalence of sexual abuse over the ages and in other cultures, and given our knowledge of the details of the circumstances in which sexual abuse occurs in our own era, that the occurrence of sexual abuse in Western post-industrial cultures has not necessarily increased significantly. The increasingly widespread disclosure of sexual abuse, and the willingness to act on it, is new. This seems to me one of the few positive aspects of the present situation. I would hypothesize that this phenomenon coincides with several other changes in our social context. Women have, in recent years, achieved significant advances in autonomy. This means not only that they can be financially independent, and therefore less trapped in abusive situations with their children; it also means that they have a voice which they can make heard to greater effect than before. Such a change will have direct and indirect effects on the social status and roles of women, and so by implication on the learning that girls acquire about their own roles in life.

The greater rights acquired by women go hand in hand with an ethos that seeks to support the rights of many groups who have been vulnerable in our culture. In particular there is increasing attention to children's rights—to life, to freedom from work and exploitation, to physical and emotional well-being. This goes together with sensitivity to anti-racism, and to the rights and points of view of disadvantaged or minority groups.

It would be naive to pretend that the legislation, international committees, and shining words from people in high places means that our culture has now changed so much that the physical and sexual abuse of children will soon be a thing of the past. This is, of course, not the case; nevertheless these evidences of a changing ethos are more than trivial and must give us all some hope.

### 3. IS PSYCHOTHERAPY THE MOST APPROPRIATE RESPONSE TO SEXUAL ABUSE?

Masson (1988) holds the view that all therapy is by its nature abusive because the power imbalance between therapist and client must, in one way or another, have a damaging effect on the quality of relationship that is possible between therapist and client. While not fully persuaded by this argument, it nevertheless seems to me important that therapists should not persuade themselves that they hold out the only hope of healing to clients (cf. also section 2 in chapter one). Abuse survivors may receive excellent help from friends, family, and self-help groups run by other survivors, and many do so without ever approaching a professional therapist. The problem in coming to a therapist for help is that you have to define yourself as someone with a problem. It is hard for clients to assess the quality and likely "fit" of a therapist before starting therapy, and once in therapy it can be hard to leave without acquiring a damaging label. Because someone who comes into therapy is, by definition, at that point unsure of herself, it can be difficult for a survivor to recognize a situation where she is likely to be more abused than helped.

It strikes me as significant that, in my own clinical practice, I have seen few survivors who defined themselves as lesbian. A significant number of the male survivors who come for therapy do define themselves as homosexual, or define their worry that they might be homosexual as part of the reason for seeking therapy. They might, for example, see the fact that they were abused by a man as having the effect of determining their sexual orientation.

Going to sources of information other than the clinical, for example lesbian feminist fiction, would suggest that significant numbers of abuse survivors have made a sexual choice that allows them to place their love and trust in other women, not in men (cf. also Jehu, 1988). Does this suggest that these women do not require the help of therapists because their cultural group provides all the help they might need in dealing with the effects of abuse?

## 4. SHOULD ADULT SURVIVORS BE ENCOURAGED TO DISCLOSE ABUSE?

This is a question that, in my experience, comes up more often in workshops than in therapy, and may reflect the preoccupation of therapists with their statutory role. However, where the abuser is known to be alive and in contact with children, the survivor may feel a moral responsibility to act to protect those children. Where survivors have brought that question to us we have indicated our willingness to support them through the various steps that disclosure may involve; this might include meetings with members of the extended family. This attitude is taken by many other practitioners, e.g. Jehu (1988).

## 5. CAN ALL ABUSE SURVIVORS BE HELPED?

Therapists notoriously have difficulty in working with situations that involve tragedy of the sort that cannot be resolved neatly. When dealing with abuse it is important for therapists to acknowledge the limitations of their skills, and the fact that clients may have had experiences that take them to the extremes of knowledge of the cruelties that human beings are capable of inflicting on one another. Naive optimism on the part of the therapist is unlikely to be helpful to a client who is struggling to come to terms with extreme experiences.

Factors that affect the degree of difficulty in achieving a therapeutic resolution will include questions such as how long the abuse continued, what acts it involved, who the abuser was, and how the abuse was stopped. For example, a survivor who was able at some point to put a stop to the abuse, e.g. because she was older and felt more confident, or because of a change in circumstances, will have had a greater experience of autonomy than someone who experienced herself as a helpless victim throughout her life.

The crucial point for a therapist would seem to be a willingness to make the journey with the client, and to accept the client's knowledge of what can be achieved. As one client said: "I still sometimes feel depressed, and alien, as if I'm different from everybody else. I think this will always stay with me, but now I'm able to keep that inside, and know that the feeling will go away again. I don't let it affect my ordinary life." This client, like a holocaust survivor, had good reason to know how bleak life could be; the achievement was to be able to live a life, together with others, that held much happiness as well as occasional memories of the events of her childhood.

## 6. WHAT IS THE FAMILY?

"It is important to remember that the family is an ideal model of what domestic groups should be, not a description of their general or normal features. . . . The internal structure of the family is based on two distinctions, each of which contains a form of superiority and justifies the exercise of authority. The division between the generations gives parents authority over children and the distinction between genders gives males superiority over females" (La Fontaine, 1990, p. 187).

Family therapists have often been accused of being in the business of maintaining the family, come what may. All therapists could usefully examine the degree to which their work, and their position within the socially sanctioned "mental health" field, constrains their freedom to think about the abuses and anomalies that are glossed over when the global term "the family" is used. We are increasingly aware of how the family may embody inequities in regard to some of its members; it is not simply a unit, in which all the parts are equally well served. We may be less aware of the extent to which, in Western industrialized culture, the nuclear family has become a closed unit, not amenable to monitoring within a community network, as families may be in other cultures. Just as a therapist needs to be aware of her own values and those of her culture in relation to gender relationships, the use and abuse of power and authority, and so on, she also requires an alertness to the functioning and aberrations of "the family".

## 7. WHAT IS A THERAPIST'S RESPONSIBILITY FOR SOCIAL CHANGE?

This is another hot potato, and therapists who draw too many meta-contextual conclusions from their work may be advised by their colleagues to be like shoemakers and to "stick to their last", and not develop delusions of grandeur in the search for "world therapy".

On the one hand, every adult survivor who is enabled to free herself from the adverse effects of her abuse, who brings up her children in a manner that ensures they will not be abused, is likely to make a difference to those with whom she comes into contact; this means that the therapeutic work will have an impact on the survivor's life, as well as a preventative influence on her environment. This would then support the idea that therapists, like ecologists, would do well to think globally but to act locally.

On the other hand, one of my earliest teachers told a story:

Once upon a time there was a woman sitting on a river bank. She saw that there were large numbers of children floating down the river. Some had already drowned, some were managing to struggle to the bank unaided, and others were sinking fast. Of course she leapt into the river and helped those who were not yet dead, but also not managing to get out by themselves. However, as soon as she got a breathing space she ran up-river to see who was pushing them in, and to put a stop to it.

# NOTES

1. I follow Eisler's usage (1988) of *androcratic*, i.e. "ruled by men" as preferable to *patriarchal*, i.e. "ruled by the father".

2. What I mean, of course, is "when we first knowingly started working with abuse survivors"; or, when we first started doing therapy in which the agreed focus was the effects of sexual abuse. I assume that other therapists who, like me, have been seeing clients in psychotherapy for more than ten years can think back with hindsight to clients who might have been trying to assess whether we would be able to hear them if they talked about having been sexually abused. The answer, by and large, was that we were not able to notice the tentative signals clients put out, and which would stand out for us now. And if they had spoken, who knows whether we would have been willing to believe them? If this seems too sweeping, look back at the "explanations" in vogue (until recently, and still current in much of mainstream psychotherapy) for behaviours such as anorexia, running away from home, self-mutilation,"hysterical" phenomena, underachievement, "schizophrenia", etc. etc., any of which now would make us at least include the possibility of abuse in

our hypothesizing. It is a useful example of the way in which one's construction of the world and "reality" can constrain what one can and cannot perceive. We might do well to ask what else we are not hearing or seeing now.

3. In a study reported by Armsworth (1989), 23% of incest survivors reported having been further sexually victimized by therapists, and a further 23% report "other forms of victimization or exploitation". Readers who have remained unaware of the degree of abuse perpetrated by therapists should read Masson (1988) and Chessler (1972).

4. This is an important point, and it is borne out by the views of those working with rape and sexual abuse survivors. The act of imposing unwanted sexual attentions on another seems to have very little to do with sexuality, in the sense of erotic excitement or attachment, and a great deal to do with hatred and the assertion of power (cf. also La Fontaine, 1990).

5. The therapist in this case was Bebe Speed, and I was involved as consultant.

# BIBLIOGRAPHY

Andersen, Tom (1987). Reflecting teams: Dialogue and meta-dialogue in clinical work. *Family Process, 26* (4), 415–428.

Armsworth, Mary Witham (1989). Therapy of incest survivors: Abuse or support? *Child Abuse and Neglect, 13,* 549–562.

Bass, Ellen & Thornton, Louise (Eds.) (1983). *I Never Told Anyone: Writings by Women Survivors of Child Sexual Abuse.* New York: Harper & Row.

Bateson, Gregory (1980). *Mind and Nature: A Necessary Unity.* Glasgow: Fontana/Collins.

Bentovim, Arnon; Elton, Ann; Hildebrand, Judy; Tranter, Marianne; & Vizard, Eileen (Eds.) (1988). *Child Sexual Abuse within the Family: Assessment and Treatment. The Work of the Great Ormond Street Team.* London: Wright.

Berger, John (1972). *Ways of Seeing.* London: BBC Publications/Penguin Books.

Blackwell, Richard D. (1990). Testimony and psychotherapy. A comment on Buus and Agger: The testimony method. *Refugee Participation Network, 7.*

Blake-White, Jill & Kline, Christine Madeline (1985). Treating the dissociative process in adult victims of childhood incest. *Social Casework: The Journal of Contemporary Social Work,* 394–403.

Booth, Philip (1988). The use of hypnosis in the recovery of memories of childhood sexual abuse. Paper presented to the First European Conference of Traumatic Stress Studies, Lincoln, U.K.

Booth, Philip (1990). La situation de l'hypnose en Angleterre. Paper presented to "Congress: 101 years after", La Société Francaise d'Hypnose, Paris.

Buus, Soren, & Agger, Inger (1988). The testimony method: The use of therapy as a psychotherapeutic tool in the treatment of traumatized refugees in Denmark. *Refugee Participation Network, 3.*

Campbell, David & Draper, Rosalind (Eds.) (1985). *Applications of Systemic Family Therapy: The Milan Approach.* London/New York: Grune & Stratton.

Cecchin, Gianfranco (1987). Hypothesizing, Circularity and Neutrality Revisited: An invitation to curiosity. *Family Process, 26* (4), 405–413.

Chessler, Phyllis (1972). *Women and Madness.* New York: Doubleday.

Courtois, Christine A. (1988). *Healing the Incest Wound: Adult Survivors in Therapy.* New York/London: W. W. Norton.

Cox, Brenda (1990). Systemic work with individual adult survivors of child sexual abuse. Dissertation submitted to The Family Institute, Cardiff, towards the University of Wales Diploma in Family Therapy.

Dolan, Yvonne (1989). "Only once if I really mean it". Brief treatment of a previously dissociated incest case. *Journal of Strategic and Systemic Therapies, 8* (4), 3–5.

Durrant, Michael & Kowalski, Kate (1990). Overcoming the effects of sexual abuse. In: Michael Durrant & Cheryl White (Eds.), *Ideas for Therapy with Sexual Abuse.* Adelaide, Australia: Dulwich Centre Publications.

Dworkin, Andrea (1990). *Mercy.* London: Secker & Warburg.

Eisler, Riane (1988). *The Chalice and the Blade: Our History, Our Future.* San Francisco, CA: Harper & Row.

Erickson, Milton H. & Rossi, Ernest L. (1976). *Hypnotic Realities.* New York: Irvington.

Finkelhor, David (1984). *Child Sexual Abuse: New Theory and Research.* New York: Free Press.

Finkelhor, David (1990). Social and cultural factors in child sexual abuse. Paper presented at the 8th International Congress on Child Abuse and Neglect, September 1990.

Freud, Sigmund (1896). The aetiology of hysteria. *S.E., 3,* p. 203.

Frude, Neil (1985). The sexual abuse of children in the family. *Medicine and Law, 4*, 463–472.

Frude, Neil (in press). Child Sexual Abuse: Themes and Deviations. Review for the *British Journal of Psychology*.

Furniss, Tilman (1991). *The Multi-Professional Handbook of Child Sexual Abuse: Integrated Management, Therapy, & Legal Intervention*. London: Routledge.

Gil, Eliana (1988). *Treatment of Adult Survivors of Childhood Abuse*. Walnut Creek, CA: Launch Press.

Gilbert, Lucia A. (1980). Feminist therapy. In: Annette M. Brodsky & Rachel T. Hare-Mustin, *Women and Psychotherapy: An Assessment of Research and Practice*. New York: Guilford Press.

Gilligan, Carol (1987). *In a Different Voice: Essays on Psychological Theory and Women's Development*. Cambridge, MA: Harvard University Press.

Gilligan, Stephen & Kennedy, Christine (1989). Solutions and resolutions. Ericksonian hypnotherapy with incest survivor groups. *Journal of Strategic and Systemic Therapy, 8*, 9–17.

Goldner, Virginia (1985). Warning: Family therapy may be hazardous to your health. *The Family Therapy Networker, 9* (6), 19–23.

Goldner, Virginia (1988). Generation and gender: Normative and covert hierarchies. *Family Process, 27*, 17–31.

Goldner, Virginia (1991). Feminism and systemic practice: Two critical traditions in transition. *Journal of Family Therapy, 13* (1), 95–104.

Gordon, Linda (1988). *Heroes in Their Own Lives*. New York: Viking.

Hall, Liz & Lloyd, Siobhan (1989). *Surviving Child Abuse: A Handbook for Helping Women Challenge Their Past*. New York/London: The Farmer Press.

Hare-Mustin, Rachel T. (1986). The problem of gender in family therapy theory. *Family Process, 26* (1), 15–27.

Haugaard, Jeffrey J. & Repucci, N. Dickon (1988). *The Sexual Abuse of Children: A Comprehensive Guide to Current Knowledge and Intervention Strategy*. San Francisco/London: Jossey-Bass.

Hildebrand, Judy & Forbes, Constanze (1987). Group work with mothers whose children have been sexually abused. *British Journal of Social Work, 17*, 285–304.

Hoffman, Lynn (1981). *Foundations of Family Therapy: A Conceptual Framework for Systems Change*. New York: Basic Books.

Hoffman, Lynn (1990). Constructing realities: An art of lenses. *Family Process, 29* (1), 1–12.

Humm, Maggie (1989). *The Dictionary of Feminist Theory*. Hemel Hempstead, Herts.: Harvester Wheatsheaf.

Jehu, Derek (in association with Marjorie Gazan, & Carole Klasen) (1988). *Beyond Sexual Abuse: Therapy with Women Who Were Childhood Victims*. Chichester/New York: John Wiley.

Jones, Elsa (1990). Feminism and family therapy: Can mixed marriages work? In: Rosine J. Perelberg & Ann C. Miller (Eds.), *Gender and Power in Families*. London/New York: Tavistock/Routledge.

Jones, Elsa (in press). *Family Systems Therapy: Developments in the Milan-Systemic Therapies*. Chichester/New York: John Wiley.

La Fontaine, Jean (1990). *Child Sexual Abuse*. Cambridge: Polity Press.

Lewin, Susan (1990). The myth of neutrality: Gender and family therapy. M.A. dissertation presented to The Polytechnic of North London.

Mackinnon, Catherine (1986). Preface. In: J. Masson, *A Dark Science*. New York: Farrar, Straus, Giroux.

Madanes, Cloe (1981). *Strategic Family Therapy*. San Francisco, CA: Jossey-Bass.

Madanes, Cloe (1991). *Sex, Love, and Violence: Strategies for Transformation*. New York/London: W. W. Norton.

Malan, Rian (1990). *My Traitor's Heart*. London: Vintage.

Masson, Jeffrey M. (1984). *The Assault on Truth: Freud's Supression of the Seduction Theory*. New York: Farrar, Straus, Giroux.

Masson, Jeffrey M. (1986). *A Dark Science*. New York: Farrar, Straus, Giroux.

Masson, Jeffrey M. (1988). *Against Therapy*. Fontana/Collins.

Maturana, Humberto R. (1988). Reality: The search for objectivity or the quest for a compelling argument. *The Irish Journal of Psychology, 9* (1), 25–82.

McCarthy, Imelda C. & Byrne, Nollaig O'R. (1988). Mis-taken Love: Conversations on the problem of incest in an Irish context. *Family Process, 27*, 181–199.

McGee, David; Browne, Ivor; Kenny, Vincent; McGennis, Aidan; & Pilot, James. (1984). Unexperienced experience: A critical reappraisal of the theory of repression and traumatic neurosis. *Irish Journal of Psychotherapy, 3* (1), 7–19.

Mitchell, Alanna (1985). Child sexual assault. In: Connie Guberman & Margie Wolfe (Eds.), *No Safe Place: Violence Against Women and Children*. Toronto, Ontario: The Women's Press.

Morgan, Fidelis (1989). *A Misogynist's Sourcebook*. London: Jonathan Cape.

Penfold, P. Susan & Walker, Gillian A. (1984). *Women and the Psychiatric Paradox*. Milton Keynes: Open University Press.

Penn, Peggy (1985). Feed forward: Future questions, future maps. *Family Process, 24* (3), 299–310.

Perelberg, Rosine J. & Miller, Ann C. (1990). *Gender and Power in Families*. London/New York: Tavistock/Routledge.

Pilalis, Jennie (1987). Consciousness-raising and family therapy. Paper presented to Fifth New Zealand Family Therapy Conference, Hamilton.

Rossi, Ernest L. & Cheek, David (1988). *Mind-Body Therapy: Methods of Ideodynamic Healing in Hypnosis*. New York: W. W. Norton.

Selvini Palazzoli, Mara; Boscolo, Luigi; Cecchin, Gianfranco; & Prata, Giuliana (1978). *Paradox and Counterparadox*. New York: Jason Aronson.

Selvini Palazzoli, Mara; Boscolo, Luigi; Cecchin, Gianfranco; & Prata, Giuliana (1980). Hypothesizing–Circularity–Neutrality: Three guidelines for the conductor of the session. *Family Process, 19* (1), 3–12.

Smith, Joan (1989). *Misogynies*. London/Boston: Faber & Faber.

Spender, Dale (1980). *Man Made Language*. London: Routledge & Kegan Paul.

Trepper, Terry S. & Barrett, Mary Jo (1989). *Systemic Treatment of Incest: A Therapeutic Handbook*. New York: Brunner/Mazel.